After Life

Solving Science and Religion's Great
Disagreement

Matthew O'Neil

Ockham Publishing

Published by Ockham Publishing in the United Kingdom

ISBN 978-1-83919-218-0

Cover design by Armend Meha

www.ockham-publishing.com

For my father

Acknowledgements

Thank you to my wonderful wife and our children. Your continual pushing for success, flexibility with my schedule, and assistance with reading and offering feedback was so valuable to me in this process. Thank you for always being with me and loving me unconditionally.

My colleagues Dan Arel, Joshua Kelly, and JD Brucker for offering insight, providing some valuable resources, and always keeping me grounded. I appreciate your friendships, support, and jokes during both the good times and the bad.

Robert Johnson, Sarah Hembrow, David G. McAfee, and Ockham Publishing for finding value in my writing and working tirelessly to ensure excellence in my piece. I appreciate all the effort and good humor along the way.

Contents

Prologue

On February 4, 1998, I walked into my high school, like I would any other day, into the main lobby. As I turned the corner, making my way toward my locker, I felt a strong discomfort and tightening in my chest. I remember putting my arm up against the door frame, cursing, and then nothing. In what felt like a few seconds, I recall opening my eyes and seeing white walls and a clock. It was nearly noon, but I did not understand why the clock was so wrong, as well as why my vision was fuzzy or why I suddenly was not in school.

A woman peaked at me and I heard her cry out, "*He's awake!*" My mother, I realized, was standing beside me; her hand on my shoulder.

> "*Where am I?*" I asked.
>
> "*The hospital,*" she said.
>
> "*Was it my diabetes or my heart?*"
>
> "*Your heart.*"

When I was ten years old, I was diagnosed with a heart condition — hypertrophic cardiomyopathy. It was discovered when the doctors noticed I had a heart murmur, and the x-ray that followed revealed I had excessive muscle tissue on the right side of my heart, making it three times larger than it would normally be. This gave me a fun bragging point in conversations, telling others I legitimately had a big heart, but did little else for me. It was a condition for which, as doctors explained, we would not know the full risks until I grew older. I had to give up sports and gym and take some bitter medicine. And suddenly, at the age of 14, we discovered what the big risk we were waiting for was.

My heart went into fibrillation that day at school; instead of beating, my heart went into a flutter, pounding at about three times the speed it should if I were in the middle of heavy exercise. And then it stopped. I was clinically dead for a period of time. I was fortunate, if such a word can be used to describe the circumstances, to have had this episode right outside of the nurse's office. I was promptly given CPR, by both the nurse and my own father who taught at the school I attended. An ambulance arrived and they took over; using both CPR and defibrillator paddles to resuscitate me. My mother told me later that, when she arrived at the hospital, they were all outside of my room crying, thinking I had died. A lot of people thought I had died that day and, to a degree, they were correct.

The doctors opted to implant an internal pacemaker/defibrillator into my abdomen, and the device has saved my life several times since then (though I have had it replaced twice since I was 14). I am more limited in my physical activity today than I was prior to the event, but, all things considered, being limited is a better option than being completely incapable.

One of the conversations I had after I woke up was with my older brother. He had witnessed me collapsing and sent a friend to get my father. We were both fans of the TV series *X-Files* and he jokingly asked if I remember being out of my body and visiting strange worlds or seeing any deceased family members. We shared a good, painful laugh, but I remember thinking that I saw nothing. Darkness. It was like waking from a dreamless slumber—nothing like what those paranormal investigation shows like *Unsolved Mysteries* displayed. And, aside from the uneasiness of remembering nothing, and knowing full well that I had been clinically dead, I had a strong desire to attempt to pursue other means of remembering what happened. Hypnosis, dreams, lucid writing — I was convinced that I must have seen something, but like a night where someone cannot remember what their dream was, it just escaped my memory.

I never made much of an investigation into these "suppressed" memories I was so convinced I had; instead I became more of an example to my friends that we are but fragile lives that can go at any time. However, one question became incredibly important to me after this event: what was the afterlife and how can we know the truth from fiction?

My account of dying, I would say, is very distant from what has been portrayed in popular media. It would be rare to see someone on a talk show, or in a movie, who recalls dying like waking from a dreamless sleep. Instead, we find accounts like *Heaven is for Real*, which describes a child's visit into Heaven, meeting Jesus, John the Baptist, and some deceased relatives. Or *23 Minutes in Hell* where a Protestant man is locked in a cell, encounters "beasts" that speak blasphemous languages, break his bones, tear his flesh, and then Jesus tells him to inform the world that Hell is real. Sadly, there are no books like *Purgatory is for Real* or *A Couple Minutes in Limbo*, but they might prove to be a subpar read.

These ideas and "experiences" are limited to the Abrahamic religions, or, more specifically, Christianity. There are certainly accounts by those who have experienced reincarnation, but, in our Western culture, those do not receive the same attention as the aforementioned visits to eternal paradise or punishment. In other words, one culture may have visions specific to their religion, as people in the Middle East having visions of Allah and Mohammed. However, people of the Western world will typically have visions of Jesus and other figures of the Christian faith.

What is very remarkable about these accounts is that they are not biblical accounts. They certainly contain the well-known figures; Satan, God, Jesus, John the Baptist, all those are accounted for. However, these are not the heavenly realm or place of torture as described in scripture.[1] In fact, a lot of what these accounts tell us is the subject's awareness of what the popular, contemporary idea of the afterlife is, even with points originating from the medieval era of Christendom. It is, as with most ideals perpetuated by the larger sects of these faiths, not based on the very book they claim tells them what they need to know to be good, wholesome people in this life, and what they should expect for a reward in the next. Jesus is typically white, as opposed to Middle Eastern, and will speak, if he does, in English rather than his native Aramaic.

Aside from a lack of concern for what their holy text describes, these patients' reports are also not based on what the scientific evidence says about our bodies, consciousness, and the experiences of the mind. Our bodies, and our minds, react in certain ways under certain conditions and, when we look at the claims made by those who have had these visits to, or experiences of, the afterlife, we can explain why they experienced those things. The same can be said of paranormal visits from those beyond the grave; there is science that explains what we see, and how we feel, when we have these experiences. It does not require a holy text, a religious practice, or any amount of dogma to understand these phenomena. Instead, we

---

[1] Isaiah 25:8-12, Matthew 5:17-20, Revelation 21:8, Matthew 25:46, etc.

have the hard, scientific evidence to show why we experience these things.

My hope is, with your choice to read this book, that I can help you understand how far we have strayed from the biblical authors' views of the afterlife. More than that, these concepts were not even original to them, but were taken from older traditions and adapted to fit the circumstances of the groups of people, and individuals, who wrote the books of the Hebrew Scriptures and the Christian Bible. I also hope to demonstrate that there is a rational explanation for things like feeling watched when no one is in the room with you, encounters with the deceased, and the concept of reincarnation.

It is with this that we start our journey in a comfortable spot —eternal paradise in Heaven and why the Bible says there is no such thing.

Chapter 1: Heaven

In the Hebrew Bible

Very early on in the Hebrew Bible, we see a mention of heaven. Or, to be more precise, what the authors of the Tanakh accepted as the concept of heaven. In Genesis 1:6-8 it details the creation of the "dome above the earth", in what would be the barrier between earth and the waters that eventually came and caused the flood in Genesis chapter six. In Genesis 7:11, it describes an opening in the firmament, "...and the floodgates of the heavens were opened." Similarly, in Psalm 148:4, "Praise him, you highest heavens, and you waters above the heavens!" It has been noted, however, that this Psalm uses Genesis 1 as the example, thanks to the language used.[2] In Genesis chapter one, verse eight, it states, "God called the dome 'Sky' ['Sky' derives from the Hebrew *shamayim*, or *shama*, which translates to 'heaven' or, literally, 'the high place']."[3] Further along in the chapter, at verse 20, it states, "And God said, 'Let the waters bring forth swarms of living creatures, and let birds fly above the earth across the dome of the sky [*shamayim*]."[4] This passage, and in its context up

---

[2]Rodd, C. S., "Psalms", *the Oxford Bible Commentary*, Oxford University Press, New York, NY, 2001, pg. 404

[3]Russell, Jeffrey Burton, *A History of Heaven*, Princeton University Press, Princeton, NJ, 1998, pg. 32-33

[4]Glasson, Thomas Francis, "Heaven", *the Oxford Guide to the Bible*, Oxford University Press, New York, NY, 1993, pg. 270

to verse 23, seems to be a story to rebuke other ancient Israelite, or Semitic, religious traditions, like the Mesopotamian *Enuma Elish*, as there are references to "the great sea monsters" in verse 21.[5]

Though these accounts are at the very start of the Bible, it comes from the Priestly source. In context, there are multiple sources to the authorship of Genesis, as well as the other books of the Pentateuch (the five books of Moses; Genesis, Exodus, Leviticus, Numbers, and Deuteronomy). We are able to tell the differences based on language, the name used to refer to God (one author is named "E" for Elohist, as this author referred to God as "Elohim", another is "J" because he referred to God as YHWH [Yahweh] and, as this concept was developed in Germany, YHWH is spelled with a "J" rather than a "Y").[6] This theory for the authorship also helps us explain why there are two creation stories (Genesis 1 and Genesis 3) and two flood stories (Genesis 6-9), why Abraham told others his wife is his sister (Genesis 12, 20, and 26), and why there are two accounts for Abraham sending Hagar and Ishmael into the desert (Genesis 16 and 21). The priestly account is the latest addition to the Pentateuch, the first five books of the Tanakh, dating to the end of the exile in Babylon in the sixth century BCE.[7]

What becomes strikingly obvious, while reading through the Hebrew Bible, is that heaven, or the heavens, were a realm

[5]Carr, David M., "Genesis", *the New Oxford Annotated Bible*, Fourth Edition, Oxford University Press, New York, NY, 2010, pg. 12
[6]Coogan, Michael, *the Old Testament: A Historical and Literary Introduction to the Hebrew Scriptures, Second Edition*, Oxford University Press, New York, NY, 2011, pg. 49-53
[7]Kugler, Robert, and Hartin, Patrick, *An Introduction to the Bible*, Wm. B. Eerdmans Publishers, Grand Rapids, MI, 2009, pg. 55

where only God existed. In Psalm 14:2 it reads, "The LORD looks down from heaven on humankind..." Psalm 8:3-4 even questions why God would consider the human race to be worthy of his care, let alone why they would be dominant over all creation: "When I look at your heavens...what are human beings that you are mindful of them, mortals that you care for them?"[8] These passages seem to indicate that, not only is heaven a realm that only God occupies, but it is any wonder that God would show any concern with humanity.[9] In fact, the only explicit mention of any human being brought into heaven was Elijah, at 2 Kings 2:11.[10] This was to emphasize Elijah's importance to the Jewish faith – that he could be inducted into the heavenly sphere where no other soul was permitted. Even the phrase, in verse twelve, "[t]he chariots of Israel and its horsemen" implies power that equated a full cavalry.[11] A further example of the authors of the Hebrew Scriptures emphasizing this is found in Malachi 4:5-6.

If we are to take the writings of Josephus into account, Josephus being a late first-century Jewish-Roman historian, later sects of Judaism, specifically the Sadducees, believed in realized eschatology. That meant, in essence, the end of the age was not coming but had already happened or was in progress. More than that, they believed that the soul dissipated at death. For YHWH, the Israelite God, was the God of the living, according to the Sadducees. And, more interestingly, scripture had no assurance

[8]Rodd, "Psalms", pg. 371
[9]Glasson, *Guide*, pg. 270
[10]Russell, *A History of Heaven*, pg. 30
[11]Römer, Thomas, "2 Kings", *the New Oxford Annotated Bible*, Fourth Edition, Oxford University Press, New York, NY, 2010, pg. 535

of the continuation of the soul after death.[12] Why would YHWH be concerned with the souls of the deceased?

Despite the fact that Jews clearly felt that heaven was only reserved for God, there are still clear ideas of what heaven looked like. In the book of Ezekiel, chapters 40-48, it relates the idea of heaven by describing it as a new Jerusalem. This is keeping in mind that Ezekiel wrote during the exile in Babylon during the sixth century BCE – a time when most of the prophetic literature of the Hebrew Bible, the *Nevi'im*, was written. As the Temple of Jerusalem housed the Ark of the Covenant, which was believed to contain the Ten Commandments and in some instances the staff of Aaron, Moses' brother, and some manna, it was believed to represent the presence of God. As such, the heavens, God's dwelling place, was depicted in Hebrew scripture to resemble not only Jerusalem, but a New Jerusalem. This is also combined with images of Eden, in Ezekiel's narrative, to create what Judaism would view as the most pristine residence for their God, YHWH. Although it emulated the image of the Jerusalem Temple, it is strange that, in heaven, the concept of sacrifice – the main practice of the temple on earth – is gone. The only accounts of sacrifice in the "new Jerusalem" are in Revelation and 3 Baruch – two books far removed from the date of the written Hebrew scriptures. Even Daniel, the very latest book, was added in the second century BCE.[13]

Aside from heaven being a dome above the earth, and God's dwelling place, it was not assigned much more

---

[12]McDannell, Colleen, and Lang, Bernhard, *Heaven: A History, Second Edition*, Yale University Press, New Haven, CT, 2001, pg. 19-20
[13]Russell, *A History of Heaven*, pg. 31

significance than that in regards to celestial spheres or the afterlife. And the earliest accounts of biblical belief seem to imply that there was no existence after death.[14] Later traditions, like those found in 1 Kings 8:27, felt that the heavens could not contain God; as the faith developed, so did the view that God was far more transcendent than previous generations held. Though prior generations held that God's dwelling place on earth was the Jerusalem Temple, the author of 1 Kings emphasizes that God does not live in the temple, but, instead, in heaven where he receives the prayers of those in the Temple.[15] Heaven as the final resting place for the followers of YHWH, as a matter of fact, is not found anywhere in the Hebrew Bible. Instead, as developed by later tradition thanks to the Hellenization of the Jews, we find the deceased descending into the earth. They found an afterlife in the pit known as Sheol.[16]

Sheol

Many people in the ancient world, the one occupied by the Israelites and others, held the belief that there was a three layer level to the physical and spiritual world. Humans resided in the earthly realm, God was located in the area above the heavens in the celestial sphere, and the dead lived in the netherworld.[17] Such a view is reflected in Genesis 42:38, with Jacob and Reuben, "If harm should befall [my son] on the journey you are taking, then you will bring my grey hair down to Sheol in

---

[14]Raphael, Simcha Paull, *Jewish Views of the Afterlife, Second Edition*, Rowman and Littlefield Publishers, Lanham, MD, 2009, pg. 50
[15]Römer, Thomas, "1 Kings". *the New Oxford Annotated Bible*, Fourth Edition, Oxford University Press, New York, NY, 2010, pg. 503
[16]Glasson, *Guide*, pg. 270
[17]McDannell and Lang, *Heaven: A History*, pg. 1

sorrow." This also mirrors Genesis 37:35, "No, I shall go down to Sheol to my son, mourning." And Numbers 16:30-33 reads, "So they and all that belonged to them went down alive to Sheol..."[18] The Hebrew Bible, as it appears, does not have a view of separation, at least at this stage, for separate realms of the land beyond for the righteous and wicked.[19] Throughout the Hebrew Bible, there are three different names synonymous with Sheol: *Abbadon*, which means "ruin" or "destruction," is used four times through all of Hebrew scripture in Psalm 88:11, Job 26:6, Job 28:22, and Proverbs 15:11. *Bor*, meaning "the pit," is seen in Isaiah 14:15, 24:22, and Ezekiel 26:20. And *shakhat*, Hebrew for "corruption," is used in Isaiah 38:17. It should be noted that, in most English translations, there is rarely a distinction made between *bor* and *shakhat*, suggesting that there is similarity in the meaning of the two words.[20]

Life in Sheol appeared rather dark and gloomy, if we look at the Hebrew Scriptures for perspective. Psalm 88:3-12 reads, "I am counted among those that go down to the pit [Sheol]; I am like one without strength...You have put me in the lowest pit, the darkest depths..." Of all the Psalms, this one is the darkest, but it also provides us with the clearest images of Sheol – beyond the care of God, darkness, forgetfulness, and silence from God when begged for help.[21] Isaiah 38:18 reads similarly, "For Sheol cannot praise you, death cannot sing your praise; those who go down to the Pit [Sheol] cannot hope for your faithfulness." And, more explicitly, in Ecclesiastes 9:10,

---

[18]Pitard, Wayne T., "Afterlife and Immortality", *the Oxford Guide to the Bible*, Oxford University Press, New York, NY, 1993, pg. 15

[19]Carr, "Genesis", pg. 64

[20]Raphael, *Jewish Views*, pg. 54

[21]Rodd, "Psalms", pg. 391

"Whatever your hand finds to do, do it with your might; for there is no work or thought or knowledge or wisdom in Sheol, to which you are going." This is included in a passage that also states, "...the same fate comes to everyone...The living know that they will die, but the dead know nothing; they have no more reward, and even the memory of them is lost." The Book of Daniel says Sheol is a land of dust (12:2), and Job says it is one of disorder (10:22), it is below the sea (26:5) and without light (10:21). While these perspectives share some similarities, they also have some markedly differing perspectives on the view of the dead and the afterlife.

Sheol was not an idea that was original to the Jewish faith. Judaism took the idea, of a common dwelling for the dead, from Greco-Roman beliefs. It certainly was not the first concept that Judaism took from them, much like how the concept of the Garden of Eden parallels the golden age of Saturn, and it certainly would not be the last.[22] If we read the *Homeric Hymn* to Demeter, [23] one of several collections of Homeric Hymns written in the seventh and sixth centuries BCE, [24] we see a shared idea between this piece, at line 16 and in the aforementioned Numbers 16, "And the roads, leading up every which way, opened up under her." The following line makes mention of the abode of Hades, in this circumstance Hades is the god of the underworld rather than the actual name of the

---

[22]Russell, *A History of Heaven*, pg. 18

[23]Nagy, Gregory, translator, *Homeric Hymn to Demeter*, the University of Houston,

[24]Burkert, Walter, "Kynaithos, Polycrates, and the Homeric Hymn to Apollo", *Arkturos: Hellenic Studies Presented Bernard M. W. Knox on the Occassion of His 65th Birthday*, Walter de Gruyter, Berlin, Germany, 1979, pg. 53-62

location, being the final destination to "many". However, at line 347, Hades is referred to as "King of the dead!" Even in this hymn, the domain of Hades is referred to as "the realms of dark mist underneath," which is reciprocated in the Book of Job 10:21-22, "...before I go, never to return, to the land of gloom and deep darkness, the land of gloom and chaos, where light is like darkness." This section is prefaced by a thought that comes from other ancient Near-Eastern sports: comparing Yahweh to a king and himself to a lion as, in royal sports, a king would hunt ferocious beasts.[25] So, as the concepts of the afterlife are not native to the Israelite faith, neither are the metaphors that the characters in the stories use.

As the concept of the afterlife developed, Sheol happened to turn into a depressing concept – even going so far as to say that the dead existed, not only without strength, but without consciousness, either.[26] This does not mean it was a place of punishment; on the contrary, being in Sheol was amoral. Though it was believed to be beyond the care of Yahweh, it was similar to the Greek view of Hades, the underworld in *the Iliad and the Odyssey*: people who were there were neither good nor bad.[27] In an Israelite mock-dirge used in Isaiah 14:4-21, a story is told of a king that tyrannized his vassals and ended up in Sheol, covered in mud and worms.[28] Job 3:11-19 even says, "Why did I not die at birth...I would be asleep, then I would be at rest with kings and counselors of the earth...There the wicked cease from troubling, and there the weary are at rest...The small and the

---

[25] Crenshaw, James L., "Job", *the Oxford Bible Commentary*, Oxford University Press, New York, NY, 2001, pg. 339

[26] Pitard, "Afterlife and Immortality", pg. 16

[27] Raphael, *Jewish Views*, pg. 53

[28] Dannell and Lang, *Heaven: A History*, pg. 6

great are there, and the slaves are free from their masters." What is interesting to note, as before, is that there are other ancient Near Eastern beliefs embedded into this section. When the authors write about Leviathan, the sea monster, in verse eight, there are parallels between Leviathan and Tiamat, from Mesopotamia. Lotan and Yamm from the Ugaritic faith would also be examples of similar myths.[29] Once again, these concepts are almost copied and pasted from other ancient beliefs that developed in the same region.

Sheol also appears to model itself after the Babylonian place of the dead, Aralu. Babylonians believed Aralu to be located below the earth, as the Israelites believed Sheol to be, and we can see that in the aforementioned passages. Aralu was also believed to be a cavern, the word to which Sheol translates in English, with gates at the entrance, similar to what Job 16:16 and 38:17 describes, "Will we go down to the gates of death...Have the gates of death been revealed to you, or have you seen the gates of deep darkness?".[30] The Babylonians' view of Aralu and the gates is seen in a poem describing Ishtar's descent into Aralu,

> To the house whence those who enter do not return,
> To the road from which there is no path leading back,
> To the house in which those who enter have no light,
> Where dust is their nourishment, clay is their food.
> They do not see light, they dwell in darkness...

---

[29]Crenshaw, "Job", pg. 335
[30]Jastrow, Morris, *the Religion of Babylonia and Assyria*, the Athenaeum Press, Boston, MA, 1898, pg. 606

On door and lock dust has settled. [31]

Babylonians also believed Aralu was a land of no return, like Job 7:9 repeats, "...one who goes down to the grave does not return." And, similarly to the ideas reflected in Psalm 88, as well as Isaiah 14:9-10, life in Aralu was full of weakness and silence, to the point where the dead could not even praise their deity.[32] Given what we have explored already with some of these books from the Hebrew Bible, it should come as no surprise to find these parallels.

Mesopotamians held that a goddess, Ereshkigal, ruled the underworld, called Cutha. Also associated with the Mesopotamians is the "land of no return", or *kurnugia*, the description of which seems to match the one of Sheol in Job 10:20-21.[33] In Mesopotamian myth, there is a recollection of a visit to the heavenly realm of the gods but, similar to the idea of Sheol in the Hebrew Bible, it is a realm strictly for the gods. The story of Adapa, a Semitic Dante, if you will, that was written in the 14th century BCE, [34] is a narrative from a first-person perspective about a mortal man ascending into the heavens and convincing the god Anu of his merits. Adapa is offered food and drink, which would give him immortality, but he declines. That is what curses humanity, according to the story, to a mortal life. Regardless, this story and others, including an epic about the King of Kish, Etana, and *the Descent of Inanna*, all describe a visit

---

[31]Nordell, Philip Augustus, *Preparations for Christianity, Volume 1*, Scribner Press, New York, NY, 1910, pg. 18-19

[32]Jastrow, *Babylonia*, pg. 606

[33]Raphael, *Jewish Views*, pg. 53

[34]Dalley, Stephanie, *Myths From Mesopotamia: Creation, the Flood, Gilgamesh, and Others*, Oxford University Press, New York, NY, 2009, pg. 182

to, and acknowledgement of, the land of the dead: the underworld. [35] And, much like the belief in Sheol, the underworld, according to *the Epic of Gilgamesh*, is "the house wherein the dwellers are bereft of light, where dust is their fare and clay their food."[36] This is almost a direct parallel to the end of Job 10.

Canaanites, the group of people who inhabited Israel prior to the Israelites, held a very interesting belief. Though it should be noted, the Israelites may have been a group of people that were once Canaanites.[37] It is interesting because it is a belief that is almost completely mirrored by the Israelite faith. Their belief was that, after death, the soul, or *nps* meaning "soul" or "spirit" (*nefesh* in Hebrew), went to the kingdom of Mot (Hebrew *mavet*), who was also called "Death".[38] The Israelites believed that, once a person was dead, they were cut off from Yahweh's presence by entering the underworld. This belief may have stemmed from an exilic, or even post-exilic, tradition that, while on foreign soil (Babylon in the case of the exile), the Israelites could not sing God's praises.[39] As in the Book of Sirach (Ecclesiasticus, a book of the apocrypha), 17:28, "From the dead, as from one who does not exist, thanksgiving has ceased; those who are alive and well sing the Lord's praises." A similar concept is found in several passages in the Hebrew Bible, including Pslam 6:5, 30:9,

---

[35]Segal, Alan F., *Life After Death: A History of the Afterlife in the Religions of the West*, Doubleday, New York, NY, 2005, pg. 103-107, 110, iBooks Edition

[36]McDannell and Lang, *Heaven: A History*, pg. 9

[37]Tubb, Jonathan N., "Canaanites" (British Museum People of the Past) and Mark Smith in The Early History of God: Yahweh and Other Deities of Ancient Israel, 1998, pg. 16

[38]Segal, *Life After Death,* pg. 155

[39]McDannell and Lang, *Heaven: A History*, pg. 10

88:10-12, 115:17-18, Isaiah 38:18, and Baruch (another apocryphal text) 2:17. For the author of Sirach, this may indicate a level of urgency for the reader, or those in the church to which the book is read, to repent. Lack of an afterlife may also be why the author of the Wisdom of Solomon felt it was necessary to lead a good life; if there is no afterlife, the only chance you get to welcome God's good graces was in this mortal life. [40] The inability to praise Yahweh, or the ability to do it only while alive, may also explain the practice of burying the dead, as it was an act to block the view of the celestial god, or gods, and brought the dead into contact with the lowest dominion.[41] So, the dead answered to, or worshipped, the infernal gods of the underworld, and Death himself: Mot.

Now, it is not only the Canaanite faith from which Mot is derived; Mot is also present in the Ugaritic belief of the afterlife. Mot is, to be more precise, a Semitic deity that personified death. The Semitic people are a large collection of groups of communities in southwestern Asia – they include, but are not limited to, the Hebrews, Canaanites, Arabs, Akkadians, and Phoenicians.[42] So, being that the Canaanites, Hebrews, and the people of Ugarit (which is now an area of northern Syria), were all Semitic people, it makes sense that there is overlap in beliefs, not just inclusive of deities and the afterlife.

---

[40]Collins, John J., "Ecclesiasticus, or the Wisdom of Jesus Son of Sirach", *the Oxford Bible Commentary*, Oxford University Press, New York, NY, 2001, pg. 679
[41]Dannell and Lang, *Heaven: A History*, pg. 5
[42]"Semite", *the Random House Dictionary*, http://dictionary.reference.com/browse/semite, 2015, retrieved January 29, 2015

Mot is also found in the Book of Job 18:13, where it reads, "By disease their limbs are consumed, the firstborn of Mot consumes their limbs." There is no surviving text of "the firstborn of Mot" in any ancient Near Eastern works, but Ereshkigal, the goddess of the underworld in Mesopotamian mythology, had a firstborn named Namtar, who was the god of plagues.[43] Even in Habakkuk 2:5, "They open their throats as wide as Sheol; like Mot they never have enough." In Ugaritic sources, Mot is the son of 'El (meaning "god"); the Israelite god Yahweh is referred to as "'El" numerous times in Hebrew scripture, like in 2 Samuel 22:31, 33-48, Genesis 14:18-20, and Psalm 89:6. Mot was also an adversary to the rain god Baal, as Mot, at least in Canaanite myth, was a deity that not only ruled the underworld, but represented all that was in opposition to life. In this case, Mot was also a god of drought. Canaanites lived in an area that had no rivers or streams, and so they had to pray to Baal for rainfall to provide healthy crops and water for livestock. It is because of this, that in the Hebrew Bible, we find the story of Elijah who battles with the prophets of Baal at 1 Kings 18. This is actually a story taken from Canaanite myth; Baal and Mot are in a battle to see who is the more powerful deity as God is battling with the prophets of Baal to prove his superiority. There is a drought, which in Canaanite myth is the work of Mot, but Yahweh takes the blame for it in the Hebrew Bible. In verse 24, Yahweh is associated with fire and lightning, as is seen in Exodus 19 and Leviticus 9:24, both of which were connected to the god Baal.[44] In Elijah's case, God consumes the sacrifice offered to him with fire, and then replenishes the land with water. The job of two gods was done by the monotheistic,

---

[43]Crenshaw, "Job", pg. 342
[44]Römer, "1 Kings", pg. 521

or henotheistic (many gods acknowledged, only one worshipped), God of Israel.[45]

As bleak as the Israelites, and other Semitic cultures, viewed the afterlife, there was an upside. Judaism taught that, even though people may be sent to a land where there is nothing but darkness, doom, and gloom, they were still reunited with their ancestors. We see examples of this in Genesis 25:8, "Abraham breathed his last and died in a good old age, an old man and full of years, and was gathered to his people." The author(s) of 1 Kings 11:43 wrote that "[King] Solomon slept with his ancestors and was buried in the city of his father David..." Also buried in David's citadel (1 Kings 2:10) were Rehoboam (1 Kings 14:31), who was Solomon's son, Asa (1 Kings 15:24) the grandson of Rehoboam, Jehoshaphat (1 Kings 22:51) the son of Asa, and so on. The belief was that being buried in your family grave reconnected you to the society of your ancestors who had passed on before you. It was not, necessarily, a belief that a physical life ended and a spiritual one began, but that a continued existence happened in another realm.[46]

Ancestral praise and cults of the dead existed prior to, and outside of, Judaism as well. Mesopotamian myth dictated that a spiritual caretaker, *paqidu*, would watch after the ghost, *etemmu*, of the deceased. This position entailed funerary offerings, which are replicated in Judaism, and many of the traits affiliated with the Israelite practice of necromancy are reciprocated in Mesopotamian faith. Such things are found in *the Epic of*

---

[45]"Mot (Semitic god)", *New World Encylcopedia*, October 22, 2008, retrieved January 30, 2015,
http://www.newworldencyclopedia.org/entry/Mot_%28Semitic_god%29
[46]Raphael, *Jewish Views*, pg. 45-46

Gilgamesh and *the Descent of Ishtar.*[47] The people of Ugarit went even further; they constructed pipes that went into the tombs of the deceased so they could provide them with water. We have found evidence of this in archaeological digs and excavations, like the one at Ras Shamra. Blessings were also sought for their king from the dead, as seen in Ugaritic funerary text KTU 1.161. In context, it appears one king, Niqmaddu IV, was recently deceased, and they were also requesting blessings for the newly enthroned king, Ammurapi.[48] Even the Canaanites, as can be seen from excavations in the city of Gezer, which was one of the most important cities to them as a people, revered the dead and developed a custom of serving their ancestors food. Egyptians, as well, have funerary art that depicts the departed at banquet tables with food that was given to them by their living family members.[49] An example of this can be seen in images like the Stele of Chaywet, which dates somewhere between 2500-2000 BCE and is currently on display in the Seattle Art Museum.[50] In the carving is the image of a man and all the food he is buried with to provide him sustenance in the next life.

In antiquity, it was viewed that, if the dead were left regular offerings of food that they enjoyed in life, they would be happy

---

[47]Friedman, Richard Elliot, and Overton, Shawna Dolansky, "Death and Afterlife: the Biblical Silence", *Judaism in Late Antiquity: Death, Life-After-Death, Resurrection, and the World to Come in the Judaisms of Antiquity, Part Four,* Brill Publishers, Boston, MA, 2000, pg. 5, retrieved from http://tinyurl.com/nnv8cky

[48]Tsumura, David Toshio, "The Interpretation of the Ugaritic Funerary Text KTU 1.161", *Official Cult and Popular Religion in the Ancient Near East*, Heidleberg: C. Winter, 1993, pg. 41-44

[49]Raphael, *Jewish Views*, pg. 46

[50]"Number 47.64: Stele of Chaywet", *Seattle Art Museum*, 2015, retrieved January 30, 2015, http://tinyurl.com/lf36p5b

and offer blessings to the family to provide the best fate. However, if the living relatives neglected the offerings, or if the offerings were interrupted, then the deceased became angry and would not offer blessings. In later beliefs, when Sheol became a layered afterlife (more on this soon), if a family member continued to not receive venerations, they would go to the lowest levels of the underworld and, eventually, became an infernal god. It was even believed they would commit harmful acts or place curses on the family; the lives of the living would, in essence, be harmed in a dramatic way.[51]

Similarly, the living very much depended on the dead, as well as depending on their god, for success and happiness in life. Being that they lived between the two worlds, the living had to appease both Yahweh and their ancestors for prosperity. Funerary offerings of food placed near the tomb, or perhaps wine spilled out for the dead, were given with the intent to keep the dead happy and generous in their blessings. We can see such examples in Deuteronomy 26:14, "I have not eaten of it while in mourning; I have not removed any of it while unclean; and I have not offered any of it to the dead." This assumes a responsibility of the living to care for the dead, which can also be found in the Ugaritic Aqhat epic.[52]

Similar sentiments are shared in Hosea 9:4 and Jeremiah 16:6-7. And in Psalm 106:28, "Then they attached themselves to the Baal [god] of Peor, and ate sacrifices offered to the dead." The latter of the two passages is somewhat ambiguous, and perhaps implies there is some form of idol worship in the

---

[51]Pitard, "Afterlife and Immortality", pg. 16
[52]Levinson, Bernard M., "Deuteronomy", *the New Oxford Annotated Bible*, Fourth Edition, Oxford University Press, New York, NY, 2010, pg. 292

Canaanite faith, but it is a retelling of funerary offerings that were, if not practiced, at least familiar to the Israelites.[53] Ben Sirach, in The Book of Sirach, also belittles the practice; 30:18 reads, "Good things poured out upon a mouth that is closed are like offerings of food placed upon a grave." Sirach equated the practice, in subsequent verses, to idol worship, as is also told in the "Bel and the Dragon" story in the Apocrypha.[54]

While there is physical, archaeological evidence to back this up, it is difficult to determine for a number of reasons. The primary being that food is perishable and evidence of it is difficult to find at burial sites. Secondly, even in instances where it is plausible that there are remnants of food, it is difficult to tell from which section of the Semitic world the corpse originated or what faith the person may have practiced.[55] Not to derail the idea, but we need to make the honest statement about beliefs and practices in ancient Judaism to get a clear picture.

Canaanites and Israelites, despite the fact that it is difficult to confirm one hundred percent that we have archaeological finds to support the idea of funerary offerings, had places of cultic worship referred to as *bamot*, which means "high place". We have archaeological evidence of such high places, like in Tel Gezer, where Canaanites are believed to have practiced cultic worship and child sacrifice.[56] We can see examples of this in the Hebrew Bible in 1 Kings 14:23, "They also set up for themselves

---

[53]Pitard, "Afterlife and Immortality", pg. 16

[54]Collins, "Ecclesiasticus...", pg. 687

[55]Johnston, Philip, *Shades of Sheol: Death and Afterlife in the Old Testament*, InterVarsity Press, Downers Grove, IL, 2002, pg. 62-63

[56]Ngo, Robin, "The 'High Place' at Tel Gezer", *Biblical Archaeology Society*, January 30, 2015, retrieved February 2, 2015, http://tinyurl.com/o5h623t

high places [*bamot*], sacred stones, and Asherah poles on every hill and under every spreading tree."

It makes sense that Asherah was used in this passage, as she was a fertility goddess and the "pillars" mentioned were phallus shaped and were used in fertility rituals.[57] The prophet Hosea (4:1-19) actually condemned the practice of communing with the dead, as he felt it constituted Baal-worship and was a part of a smaller sect of Judaism that was viewed as heresy, or, at least, apostate Judaism. And, as the belief changed from generation to generation, the practice became synonymous with being an apostate in the seventh and sixth generation BCE.[58]

One of the better examples, at least of necromancy, in the Hebrew Bible is the example of Saul, the king of Israel before David, wishing to speak to the deceased prophet Samuel. In 1 Samuel 28:7-25, "Saul said to his servants, 'Seek out for me a woman who is a medium [*baalat eishet ob*]...'" And Saul's servants say they know of a woman medium in Endor, so they go to find her. When they do, Saul tells her to bring up Samuel, and that is exactly who appears. Samuel is then able to relay to Saul that Yahweh has given Israel to David and that Saul, and his sons, will "join" him the following day – essentially letting him know that his time on earth was up. Though this is the only story to support the idea of an actual practice of necromancy in the Hebrew Bible, the popularity of the practice can be seen in the numerous accounts that chastise and denounce the practice from the eighth to the sixth century. We see these in places like Leviticus 19:31, "Do not turn to mediums or wizards; do not

---

[57]Römer, "1 Kings", pg. 514
[58]"High Place", *the Encyclopedia Britannica: A Dictionary of Arts, Sciences, Literature and General Information, Volumes 13-14*, Encyclopedia Britannica, New York, NY, 1911, pg. 456

seek them out, to be defiled by them: I am the LORD your God." Leviticus 20:6, "I will set my face against anyone who turns to mediums...I will cut them off from their people." Deuteronomy 18:10-14, "No one shall be found among you...who casts spells, or who consults ghosts or spirits, or who seeks oracles from the dead." Isaiah 8:9-10 reads similarly. In short, we can know that necromancy was practiced; it was popular because of how frequently it is criticized, and banned from being practiced in Hebrew scriptures.

Even Saul is heavily criticized by the seventh century editor of the books of Samuel.[59] Scholarship writes that, right in the middle of the necromancy scene, in verses 3 through 19, we have an insertion by a Deuteronomic author – or one that either worked on, or was a member of the group that is responsible for, the Book of Deuteronomy. This is because of the language used, specifically at 28:7, "Seek out for me a woman who is a medium, so that I may go to her and inquire of her." This is believed to be an insertion by the Deuteronomic author to give reason for the prohibition of necromancy; that is because the language used for "inquire", *daras*, is the same used in Deuteronomy, as opposed to the Levitical phrasing *pana*, meaning "turn[ing] unto" necromancers.

In spite of that, the story itself gives heavy indication for the reader to infer that the request, and the action, is problematic for Saul. Even when approaching the woman to summon Samuel, she says to him, "Why then are you laying a snare for my life to bring about my death?" And, it can be argued, after Samuel tells Saul that he and his sons will "join" him the following day, that Saul had sealed his fate by seeking a

---

[59]Pitard, "Afterlife and Immortality", pg. 16

necromancer and communing with the dead.[60] Perhaps because calling on the dead was done, more frequently, by people in higher positions of power during rough political or economic circumstances,[61] calling on the dead was viewed as a private matter, done for personal gain. However, calling on God was a communal action; it was something done to benefit the people of a group, or tribe, rather than an individual.[62] It should be noted that, while the laws of Leviticus and Deuteronomy do not completely ban the practice, they do say that it is, in so many words, inappropriate.[63]

Just prior to the Assyrian and Babylonian exiles, in the eighth and seventh century BCE, a new religious sect surfaced that was called the "Yahweh Alone" movement. This group, breaking away from traditional religious norms both in pagan and the Jewish faiths, sought to ensure that only one god was recognized. This meant no acknowledgement of other deities from other cultures, no concept of worshipping Mot, the god of the dead, in the afterlife, and, in fact, no veneration of the dead either. Rather than henotheism, this was a true breaking away from the traditions of early Judaism into monotheism.[64] This did not help to create a more blissful afterlife, but, instead, it meant completely distancing oneself from the deceased. Despite the fact that this movement sought to eradicate the worship and

---

[60] Arnold, Bill T., "Necromancy and Cleromancy in 1 and 2 Samuel", *the Catholic Biblical Quarterly*, Catholic Biblical Association of America, Washington, DC, 66, 2004, pg. 207
[61] Ibid.
[62] McDannell and Lang, *Heaven: A History*, pg. 5
[63] Pitard, "Afterlife and Immortality", pg. 16
[64] Dever, William G., *Did God Have a Wife?: Archaeology and Folk Religion in Ancient Israel*, Wm. B. Eerdman's Publishing, Grand Rapids, MI, 2005, pg. 285

acknowledgement of other deities, believers still insisted that, in Sheol, people continue to worship Yahweh. [65] A rather depressing view: worship a deity from which you are completely removed and who cannot hear you. Considering the numerous Psalms that dictate that Sheol keeps the dead from being able to contact the living and God (6:5, 30:8-10, 88:3-12) and the five centuries it was written during, including time in the period of exile, it appears to insinuate an almost total separation from the Israelite God.[66]

The Yahweh Alone movement also banned necromancy; the ability to commune with the dead. Aside from feeling it was acknowledging others the way Yahweh should be acknowledged, necromancy was also viewed as a magical deviation and it threatened national interests, as worshipping and calling on Yahweh was a communal, political action. As such, worshipping Yahweh was something that took priority over worshipping, or communicating with, the dead.[67] We can see the condemnation of necromancy, along with child sacrifice and magic, in Deuteronomy 18:11, and Leviticus 20:27, "A man or a woman who is a medium or spiritist among you must be put to death." Even the prophets attempted to end the practice, as Isaiah writes (26:14) "They are dead, they can never live. Rephaim [the inhabitants of Sheol], they can never rise." Psalm 88:10, Job 26:5-6, and Proverbs 9:18, 21:16 all reciprocate this idea of the

---

[65]McDannell and Lang, *Heaven: A History*, pg. 10
[66]Kselman, John S., "Psalms", *the New Oxford Annotated Bible with the Apocrypha/Deuterocanonical Books*, Oxford University Press, New York, NY, 2007, pg. 775
[67]McDannell and Lang, *Heaven: A History*, pg. 7

dead being unable to help the living.[68] As such, the living should cease in their attempts to commune with the dead.

Towards the end of the eighth century BCE, the Assyrians laid siege to the northern kingdom of Jerusalem, in Samaria. When this occurred, it gave a clear opportunity for those espousing the views of the Yahweh Alone movement to voice their beliefs. Most notably, those who held strongly to these views taught others that the Assyrians were successful because the Israelites did not worship Yahweh as the one true God. And, if the Book of Job did not emphasize it enough, this was because both punishment and reward were viewed as being given in a persons, or community's, mortal life.[69]

In Job 4:6-9, Job's friend Eliphaz tells him that, in spite of Job's worship of Yahweh and following of his rules, he must have done something wrong. "It's been my experience that those who plow the soil of iniquity and those who sow the seed of trouble will reap their harvest...they are consumed by the storm that is [God's] anger." Also, in Proverbs 11:31, "If the righteous are repaid on earth, how much more the wicked and the sinner!" Likewise, because the Yahweh Alonists held such a view, clearly the punishment of the siege by the Assyrians was because of the Israelites' failing to worship Yahweh as the one, true God. But then, thanks to King Josiah in 623 BCE, Yahweh was declared the one true God of Israel and, thanks to this declaration that solidified a national acceptance of the Yahweh Alone movement, the Israelites stopped defining themselves in relation

---

[68]Raphael, *Jewish Views*, pg. 55
[69]McDannell and Lang, *Heaven: A History*, pg. 7 & 11

to their ancestors. Instead, they were then defined solely in relation to their God.[70]

At the end of the eighth century, and into the sixth, things shifted that called for a necessary change of beliefs for the Jews. Aside from the siege by the Assyrians, the Babylonians came and exiled the Israelites from their land. These events then created a concern: if Sheol was a land where everyone ended up after death, how could these cultures, these tribes of Babylon and Assyria, be welcomed in? Were the Israelites doomed to share the underworld with the people who slaughtered their people and took their promised land away from them? A new, retributive form of the afterlife was instilled into the faith. This new view ended up splitting Sheol into a multi-layered realm, where the worst of the wicked ended up in the southern-most parts.[71] We can see references to this in Isaiah 14:9 and Ezekiel 32:18, where there are threats of those who are hostile towards Israel going down "to the pit". This view also extended to those who died criminal deaths, or on the battlefield without a proper burial.[72] In the end, God would not leave his servants to be persecuted, or to die for their faith, without vindication.[73] In fact, more importantly to people of the Jewish faith, part of the switch from a dark and gloomy Sheol was, in part, to provide a reward for heroes of the faith in the next life.[74]

Around this time, and leading up to the second century BCE, we start to see use of the word "paradise" in reference to the afterlife. Prior to this time, the word "paradise" is used

---

[70]McDannell and Lang, *Heaven: A History*, pg. 10
[71]Raphael, *Jewish Views*, pg. 60-61
[72]McDannell and Lang, *Heaven: A History*, pg. 6
[73]Glasson, "Heaven", pg. 270
[74]Russell, *A History of Heaven*, pg. 18

sparingly in the Hebrew Bible. Originally, the word is Persian, *pairidaeza*, and meant "enclosed garden," which was something given or belonging to Persian kings. Outside of the Garden of Eden story, it is used only three other times, not in reference to Eden, including at Ecclesiastes 2:5, "I made myself gardens and parks [p*ardes,* the Hebrew *for "paradise"*], and planted in them all kinds of fruit trees." Also at Nehemiah 2:8, "...and a letter to Asaph, the keeper of the king's forest [*pardes*]..." It is because of the previously mentioned need to distance the wicked from the righteous that, as a lower level of Sheol was created, so was the blessed part of Sheol, called *pardes*, or "paradise". It is thanks to the Septuagint, the Greek [mis]translation of the Hebrew Bible that Eden, as well as the blessed part of the netherworld, *paradeisos*, or Paradise, was made around the second century BCE.[75]

Certainly there was further development of the concept of heaven, paradise, and joining said paradise to be in the presence of Yahweh, but we must take a quick turn down a different road for the time being. We will return to this point when we discuss the concept of resurrection.

Heaven in the New Testament

Around the time Jesus was alive, the author(s) of a book called 2 Enoch wrote of the protagonist, after whom the book is named, coming into the presence of God. At 22:1-10, God tells his angels, inclusive of Michael the Archangel, "Let Enoch join in and stand in front of my face forever...Go and extract Enoch from his earthly clothing. And anoint him with my delightful oil, and put him into the clothes of my glory." This passage is

---

[75]Russell, *A History of Heaven*, pg. 31

intriguing as, if we look at Genesis 32:22-32 and Exodus 33:20, we know that it was believed no one could see the face of God and live. Later in the book, at 37:2, Enoch's face is made so bright that no one is able to look at it. Similarly, in the Book of Sirach, written about one hundred years or so prior to 2 Enoch, at 45:1-5, Moses, who we are told dies alone and in an unknown location (Deuteronomy 34:5-6), is made "equal in glory to the holy ones, and [God] made him great, to the terror of his enemies." So, not only are we seeing a transition from the Jewish belief of a dark, gloomy afterlife, where souls, if one wishes to call them that, are weak and ignorant, to a revitalized, powerful belief— now humans are brought into the heavenly realm, sometimes still alive, and given remarkable powers.[76]

And it is not just the patriarchs, or other dominant figures, of the faith that are given special treatment. In 2 Baruch, a Jewish text written around the same time as the gospels, stated that the righteous transformed "into the splendor of angels...for they will live in the heights of the world and they will be like the angels and be equal to the stars...and the excellence of the righteous will then be greater than that of the angels." Humans, specifically the righteous, were given the privilege of becoming powerful angels. What is more, they are given divine privilege and, as people in antiquity believed, those that were given higher glory as angels were seen as the stars in the sky.[77]

What should be realized, in regards to a more modern understanding of heaven and joining God in paradise, is this concept is rather absent from the New Testament accounts.

---

[76]Ehrman, Bart D., *How Jesus Became God: the Exaltation of a Jewish Preacher from Galilee,* Harper Collins, New York, NY, 2014, pg. 60, Kindle Edition
[77]Ehrman, *How Jesus Became God*, pg. 59

And what is very important to understand is that the authors of the books of Christian scripture were Jewish—more than that, they were Jewish apocalypticists. What was different between these Jews of the Jesus movement, when compared to the Jews of other sects, was that Jesus was viewed as the Messiah in what would eventually become the religion known as Christianity. Noted passages, to back this concept, are ones like Matthew 5:12, "Do not think that I have come to abolish the [Jewish] law or the prophets; I have come not to abolish but to fulfill." In Romans 11:1,Paul of Tarsus explains that he was from the tribe of Benjamin, and Acts 23:6 tells us that Paul was a Pharisee. Even in the Gospel of Luke, in 20:38, we find similar sentiments to those held by the authors of the Hebrew Bible, "Now he is God not of the dead, but of the living..." This mirrors the idea of Sheol being separated from Yahweh.

In the New Testament, as in the Hebrew Bible, the word "heaven" was used frequently in reference to the sky. Mark 13:25, "...the stars will fall from the sky, and the heavenly bodies will be shaken." Ephesians 4:10 mirrors the concept of heaven as the sky, "He who descended is the same one who ascended far above all the heavens, so that he might fill all things." In Matthew 28:18,Jesus states that "All authority in heaven and on earth has been given to me." But this is in regards to Jesus having the omnipresence of Yahweh; much the same as God was viewed as the only one who could heal the sick or forgive sins (Matthew 9:1-8 is a good example), Jesus took on that divine authority. It does not mean that heaven became a place for the dead; just that Jesus could exhibit the power of God from heaven.[78]

---

[78]Glasson, "Heaven", pg. 270

Further, in Luke 15:18 and 21, we find the following: "I will get up and go to my father, and I will say to him, 'Father, I have sinned against heaven and before you'...Then the son said to him, 'Father, I have sinned against heaven and before you; I am no longer worthy to be called your son.'" This is from the parable of the Prodigal Son, and there is something interesting we must be aware of. In both instances, we see the protagonist admits to having sinned against "heaven and before you". This is from an old Jewish observance; the name of God, and God himself, was shown reverence by not saying his name and, often at times, using substitutes. A clear example is in Exodus 3:14, when God instructs Moses to go address the Israelites on his behalf, "God said to Moses, 'I AM WHO I AM. This is what you are to say to the Israelites: "I AM has sent me to you."'" As such, in later traditions like in Luke, other words indicative of God and his grandeur were used as substitutes. In this case, it is "heaven;" so the son is saying he has sinned before God and his father— not heaven.[79]

What is striking is how sparingly the word "heaven" is used in connection to the afterlife. While the biblical authors encourage and reassure their readers with a blissful eternity, continuing the idea left off from those from the era of the exile, it is not in connection to the heavenly realm. In Mark 10:21, Jesus tells the rich young man to sell all he owns and he will have "treasure in heaven." It appears Jesus is attempting to make a case for the modern understanding of what heaven is, but it is a concept of a gift coming *from* heaven to earth. It is the coming kingdom of God to earth.[80] This goes back to the idea of the authors being apocalypticists; in other Jewish apocalyptic

[79]Glasson, "Heaven", pg. 271
[80]Glasson, "Heaven", pg. 270

literature, when Adam and Eve were expelled from Eden, it meant a loss of the presence of God on earth. So to seek redemption, then, meant bringing back the paradise of Eden and a return of God's presence on earth. This also meant, when the world ended, that the righteous would return to the new Eden. In fact, Jesus even uses apocalyptic imagery to describe what the new Eden would look like in Matthew 11:5, which is almost verbatim what Isaiah 35:5 says about the blind seeing, the deaf hearing, and the lame walking.[81]

Eden was equated with paradise around the second century BCE, thanks in large part to the Septuagint, as mentioned before. This became the place for the faithful, the righteous. Central to this idea was the concept of Jerusalem being the new Eden. As King David had brought the Ark of the Covenant into Jerusalem, it meant that God's dwelling place on earth was *in* Jerusalem. Thanks to the Greek translation of the Hebrew Bible, as well as the concept of a new Eden, or renewed earth, it meant that paradise in the afterlife was located on earth. Not in the earth, as previous generations felt with Sheol, but in the city of Jerusalem.[82] This is seen in Isaiah 51:3 in the Hebrew Bible, "The LORD will surely comfort Israel again and will look with compassion on all her ruins; he will make her deserts like Eden." Even in Isaiah 58:11, "You will be like a well-watered garden [Eden], like a spring whose waters never fail." In the New Testament, we see this concept in the Book of Revelation. At 21:10-11, John of Patmos writes that he is carried away to a high mountain and showed "the holy city Jerusalem coming down out of heaven from God." He continued, " It has the glory of

---

[81]Shaw, Gregory, "Paradise", *the Oxford Guide to the Bible*, Oxford University Press, New York, NY, 1993, pg. 570

[82]Russell, *A History of Heaven*, pg. 31

God and a radiance like a very rare jewel, like jasper, clear as crystal." Revelation 21 is almost entirely spent describing the New Jerusalem, which resembles something that came from heaven, but is not *in* the heavenly sphere.

We do know that, according to Jesus, in the New Jerusalem there will be no marriage. In Luke 20:27-40, the Sadducees, who did not believe in the resurrection as Jesus and his followers did, ask Jesus what would happen if a woman had to marry seven subsequent brothers, as per the law of levirate marriage when a woman failed to provide offspring before a man passed away. When they met in God's kingdom on earth, they asked sarcastically, would she then be married to all seven? Jesus' quick answer is that "You are in error because you do not know the Scriptures or the power of God. At the resurrection people will neither marry nor be given in marriage; they will be like angels in heaven." While we will talk about the resurrection at a later point, it is important to stress that they do not *become* angels in heaven, but they will be *like* angels in heaven. Heaven is, still, not linked with the afterlife, but there will be instances where characteristics of heaven will enter the paradise of which the faithful will be a part.[83]

Jesus also told stories that gave some implications of the change in the view of the world to come—including the parable of the rich man and Lazarus, in Luke 16:19-31. In this parable, Jesus describes a rich man who "feasted sumptuously" every day, and Lazarus, who was destitute and covered in sores. When Lazarus dies, he is "carried away by the angels to Abraham's bosom." There is no mention of heaven, let alone any paradise. However, there has been a shift from the concept of joining

---

[83]McDannell and Lang, *Heaven: A History*, pg. 25

ones ancestors to, now, being with one of the patriarchs of the faith. We can contribute this change, in part, to Jesus' position as anti-family. We see this in Matthew 12:46-50 when, after being told his family is looking for him, Jesus responds, "'Who is my mother and who are my brothers?' And pointing to his disciples, he said, 'Here are my mother and my brothers! For whoever does the will of my father in heaven is my brother and sister and mother.'" Perhaps it is not hard to understand Jesus' anti-family values when his own family thought he was crazy — Mark 3:21 reads, "When his family heard it, they went out to restrain him, for people were saying, 'He has gone out of his mind.'" It appeared they also took his ministry with a grain of salt, as, in John 7:5, we see that, "For even his own brothers did not believe him." When addressing them face-to-face, Jesus was not too kind. In John 2:4, at the wedding in Cana of Galilee, Jesus' mother informs him that they are out of wine. Jesus responds, "Woman, what concern is that to you and to me?" Even publicly, Jesus was not very respectful towards his mother. Luke 11:27 has a woman offer a blessing to Jesus' mother "who gave birth and nursed you." Jesus responds, "Blessed rather are those who hear the word of God and obey it."

Jesus' anti-family view was not limited to his own. Luke 12:51-53 shows a Jesus that was intent on ensuring families were divided. He is asked if he was sent to bring peace on earth, and his response is, "No, I tell you, but division...They will be divided, father against son and son against father, mother against daughter and daughter against mother, mother-in-law against daughter-in-law and daughter-in-law against mother-in-law." Jesus actually tells his followers in Matthew 19:29 that "...everyone who has left houses or brothers or sister or fathers or mother or children or fields for my sake will receive a hundred times as much and will inherit eternal life." The list goes on, but the point, I believe has been made. Especially with the last passage, Jesus has completely denied the concept of returning to one's family at death, even saying a believer should deny his or her own family in life to be granted "eternal life". As a short aside, it is helpful to remember that Jesus was also not married and had no children.[84] Instead of returning to kin, the dead now are carried to the religions heroes. This was to put focus back on God and the leaders of the faith, rather than on the continued offering of veneration to the dead. Worship of God, a public practice done for the common good, took precedence over private worship of the family, which only benefitted the individual.[85]

When we get to the writings of Paul, we still find little, if anything, about heaven. We do know that Paul was allegedly blinded by a light "from heaven," according to Acts 9:3-6. However, the author of Acts, who was also the author of Luke, writes about the ministry of Paul and his conversion like someone who only knew the apostle through oral myth. For example, Acts states that Peter preached to Gentiles at 10:27-29, but in Galatians 2:7, an authentic letter of Paul, it says Peter only preached to "the circumcised," or the Jews. Among other reasons, including the complete absence of the blinding light story from Paul's legitimate writing, it not only should be viewed as a later tradition made up by the author of Acts, but as a passage that merely states where the light came from. No other detail is provided. Paul does write, in 2 Corinthians 5:10, that "all must appear before the judgment seat of Christ, so that each may receive recompense for what has been done in the body..." But, again, there is no implication that this is in the heavenly

---

[84]McDannell and Lang, *Heaven: A History*, pg. 32
[85]McDannell and Lang, *Heaven: A History*, pg. 27

realm. Paul implies, in Ephesians 2:6, that heaven is not even a physical place—that those who acknowledge Jesus as the Messiah already sit with him in heavenly places. Paul makes it clear, however, that it is more metaphorical than literal; he writes, "...even when we were dead through our trespasses, [God] made us alive in Christ...and raised us up with him and seated us with him in the heavenly places..."[86]

Paul, very much like the gospel authors and those of the epistles, says next to nothing about a celestial paradise. The Book of Hebrews speaks of developing a country that would be like a heavenly one (11:16, 12:18-24) and says that when the end comes the heavens will be destroyed along with the earth (1:10-11) and that Jesus had passed through the heavens (4:14, 7:26). But, again, there is nothing of heaven, or the heavenly sphere, being the location where the righteous dead would reside. The closest we come is when the author of Hebrews writes that Jesus sits at the right hand of God, at 9:23-24 and 8:5.[87] Still, it is not where the faithful go when they die. There truly appears to be no single, let alone collective, idea of paradise in heaven. And this is thanks primarily to their eschatological, or end-times, view. These authors all felt the end was imminent, and this meant, not only a rebuilding of Israel as the new Eden, but a resurrection of the dead. [88] We will discuss resurrection in chapter three, but we should take notice of the one book in the New Testament that *does* mention heaven and serves as s place from which modern concepts of heaven are derived.

[86]Glasson, "Heaven", pg. 270
[87]Ibid.
[88]Russell, *A History of Heaven*, pg. 40-41

There appears to be one passage, and one that was legitimately written by Paul of Tarsus, that seems to imply a joining of Jesus in the heavenly sphere. In 1 Thessalonians 4:17, it reads, "Then we who are alive, who are left, will be caught up in the clouds together with them [those who have already died] to meet the Lord in the air; so we will be with the Lord forever." This claim has led to the concept known as "the rapture;" wherein people are suddenly zapped up into heaven to join Jesus for all eternity in paradise. We have seen it in the *Left Behind* series, as well as the recent Seth Rogan and James Franco movie "This is The End." However, it does not mean that—at least not entirely. The concept for which Paul still advocated was a paradise on earth but, by joining Jesus in heaven, they were greeting him to welcome him, and perhaps Yahweh, onto the newly heaven-conquered earth.

A title for this, usually equated with the return of Jesus, is "Parousia." There was actually a political affiliation with this word and its use. Josephus, as an example, wrote about a visit that Alexander the Great made to Jerusalem in 332 BCE. Alexander intended to pass through to Egypt with no conflict, after having conquered Damascus, Sidon, and Tyre. At the time, the high priest Jaddus was dreading the visit, but changed his mind after having received a dream in which he was told to "adorn the city with wreaths and open the gates and go out to meet them, and that the people should be in white garments." He was told, in essence, to prepare for the *Parousia* of Alexander.[89] And this does not sound too far off from what

---

[89]Kraybill, J. Nelson, *Apocalypse and Allegiance: Worship, Politics, and Devotion in the Book of Revelation*, Brazos Press, Grand Rapids, MI, 2010, pg. 174-175

Paul is saying to the Thessalonians, particularly with using the title "Lord" to refer to Jesus.

Revelation

What we might consider to be the more popular, and well known, concepts of heaven today mostly come from the Book of Revelation.[90]

To give some context behind the book: Revelation was written, very likely, during the reign of Emperor Domitian, toward the end of the first century CE. However, there is speculation parts may have been written earlier. This is because of the number 666, which is known as the "mark of the beast". When added together, 666 equals the value of Emperor Caesar Nero's name in Hebrew, who reigned from 54-68CE. In Chapter 13:3 of Revelation there is a mention of one of the beasts having a "fatal wound" that had somehow healed itself, which is believed to be alluding to Nero's suicide by slitting his own throat. John of Patmos, the author of Revelation strongly believed that Nero would return from the dead. With John being an apocalyptic Jewish Christian, combined with the sense that God would intervene soon to stop the Roman Empire, he wrote this apocalyptic text to provide reassurance to his audience, and the several churches mentioned in the letter. God is coming soon, and this is what you can expect![91]

John describes, in chapter four, entering heaven through a door into a vast chamber to see God's divine throne with God in it. Or, at least, "the one seated there looked like jasper and

---

[90]Glasson, "Heaven", pg. 271
[91]Burkett, Delbert, *An Introduction to the New Testament and the Origins of Christianity*, Cambridge University Press, Cambridge, UK, 2000, pg. 503-504

carnelian, and around the throne is a rainbow that looks like an emerald." Around the throne of God are 24 thrones for the 24 elders, possibly representing the twelve apostles and the twelve tribes of Israel. Some also think these are angelic beings; however the number 24 is the traditional number of Jewish priestly families, or those identified as priests.[92] There are also flashes of lightning and thunder, which is taken from Ezekiel 1:4, and seven lit torches for the seven spirits of God, taken from, and a combination of, Ezekiel 1:13 and Zechariah 4:2. Crystal-like sea glass is seen in front of the throne, from Ezekiel 1:22 and Exodus 24:10, as well as the four living creatures with different animal appearances, taken from Ezekiel 1:4-21, 10:1-14, and Isaiah 6:1-7. There are also similar descriptions of the animals in Exodus 25:17-22, 1 Samuel 4:4, and Psalm 80:1.[93] Very much like other places in the New Testament, there was a heavy dependence on Hebrew Scripture to emphasize, and detail, the stories written by these authors. And, perhaps, a glimmer of hope that the audience would never know or read the books from which they took these references.

For the most part, Revelation reads as metaphors and symbolism for what the author felt was the evil ways of the Roman Empire and those that worshipped false idols. Though we are given a detailed description of, at the very least, the throne of God, as well as the background music of the heavenly choir exalting Jesus (5:11-13), we do not get much of a description of the heavenly realm. Actually, when we do start getting a more precise look at the paradise in the next life, it is

---

[92]McDannell and Lang, *Heaven: A History*, pg. 39

[93]Rhodes, Erroll F., Editor, "Revelation", *the Good News Study Bible with Deuterocanonicals/Apocrypha,* American Bible Society, New York, NY, 1993, pg. 1675

when heaven joins earth. This mirrors visions from the book of 1 Enoch, a work dating from 300 BCE to the first century CE, of the merging of earthly and heavenly paradises.[94] In Revelation 21, there is a new heaven joining a new earth (Isaiah 65:17, 66:22) after the older version of the two "fled from [God's] presence and were seen no more" (Revelation 20:11). John writes, "And I saw the Holy City, the new Jerusalem, *coming down out of heaven* from God, prepared and ready, like a bride dressed to meet her husband [Emphasis my own]."Similarly, the Targum on Psalm 122:3 also made reference to a "new Jerusalem" and indicated that it would be "built in heaven".[95] While this passage is filled with imagery and terms used in other sections of the Bible (Isaiah 52:1 for "Holy City", Galatians 4:26 and Hebrews 12:22 for "new Jerusalem"), what is made abundantly clear is what we already know from earlier in the discussion—that heaven is a divine realm for God. It's important to note, though, that there are now some divine, more human-like characters in God's presence, and the afterlife will take place, not only on earth, but on the *new* earth, in the *new* Jerusalem, under the *new* heaven.[96]

What was strongly emphasized in Revelation, and likely was the very reason John of Patmos wrote the book, was how distant this new world would be removed from their contemporary society. Christians, Jewish Christians to be more precise, were a very small minority in the first century. And, due to the apocalyptic movement, as well as the pacifist position many of them took (which Dr. Candida Moss details excellently in her book *the Myth of Persecution* [Harper One, 2014]), Jewish

---

[94]Russell, *A History of Heaven,* pg. 38
[95]Russell, *A History of Heaven*, pg. 39
[96]McDannell and Lang, *Heaven: A History*, pg. 43 & 44

Christians were rather difficult to force into compliance with societal norms. This was especially problematic in a setting where it was expected, and very normal, for Roman citizens to want to take up arms to defend their country, they would even take an oath of allegiance. So, if a citizen defected or refused, the behavior was frowned upon and met with severe punishment.[97] We see a concern for this, the alleged "martyrdom" of Christianity's earliest followers, in Revelation 7:14, which describes people "wash[ing] their robes and [making] them white in the blood of the Lamb." This refers to those killed "for the faith," as well as to those who suffered as a result of the "great ordeal" under Nero, in which Nero (allegedly) blamed Christians for starting the large fire in Rome and caused the alleged persecution and public executions.[98] John wanted to show, not only a separation from the civilization to which Jews had grown accustomed, but that there would be a permanence of ecstasy and a freedom from the constraints of the world in which they lived to fully experience the presence of their god.[99]

While this was a new concept, one of experiencing joy, light without the sun, and seeing the presence of God, as well as breaking free from the limitations of the mortal coil, the idea of paradise in the heavenly realm was completely absent. A new Jerusalem, or a new paradise, is present, but humanity is not in the heavenly sphere.

[97]Moss, Candida, *the Myth of Persecution: How Early Christians Invented a Story of Martyrdom*, Harper One, New York, NY, 2014, pg. 172, Kindle Edition
[98]McDannell and Lang, *Heaven: A History*, pg. 40
[99]McDannell and Lang, *Heaven: A History*, pg. 44 & 45

After the Bible

It did not take long after the time the canonized books of the New Testament were written for more Greek-influenced philosophies of the afterlife to begin to appear in Christian circles. Among those positions were those held by Plato (428-347 BCE) and Cicero (106-43 BCE), who both held that the reward to the righteous in the afterlife was in the heavenly sphere above, not only the earth, but the stars.[100] Even Aristotle (384-322 BCE), and his view on physics, helped to create the concept of heaven and paradise being in the sky, as up was better than down. This concept was used by different Christian philosophers, including Ptolemy.[101]

Views in antiquity regarding paradise or the afterlife in heaven are mixed, to say the least. In the second century, Justin Martyr, as an example, felt that life in heaven could not be enjoyed, or achieved, by those who had died until after the great resurrection and judgment. Justin, as well as Church father Ignatius, did hope that martyrdom would grant instant access into the heavenly paradise.[102]

This was a very common view; in *the Acts of Scillitan Martys*, the character Narzalus says, upon his death, "Today we are martyrs in heaven!" Even Polycarp, the bishop of Smyrna in the second century CE, in his last prayer, says, "May I be received this day among [the martyrs] before your [God's] face." And even though Paul wrote that all face eschatological judgment (2 Corinthians 5:10), it was believed they avoided it all together.[103]

---

[100]McDannell and Lang, *Heaven: A History*, pg. 16
[101]Russell, *A History of Heaven*, pg. 22
[102]Russell, *A History of Heaven*, pg. 54-55
[103]Moss, *Myth of Persecution*, pg. 208-209

In the story "the Martyrdom of Marian and James," there is an account of a deacon named James and a reader named Marian, who were executed in 259 CE during the Valerian persecution.[104] In this story, the question is asked, "Will all of you martyrs receive equally the reward of heavenly gifts without distinction?" A fair question, and when compared to the stars in heaven (some greater than others), the answer? "...those whose victory is slower and with greatest difficulty, those receive the more glorious crown."[105]

It is difficult to tell, but the belief is a very literal one—not metaphorical, as the comparison to the stars would seem to imply. Indeed, as we can infer from Revelation 3:21, martyrs were given crowns and received seats on the throne of God. This meant an exalted status—even the possibility to have a sense of command along with God. And this view, of reward and exaltation in heaven, was a very dominant view among early Christians, despite Appollonius of Rome's position of "living a good life," as he wrote before his martyrdom. Indeed, there was a more central focus on doing good deeds for the reward of an afterlife in paradise, whether it was on earth or in the heavens, rather than being good for goodness' sake.[106]

Irenaeus, a second century Church father, also held a newer belief. In *Against Heresies* (5.36.1-2), Irenaeus advocated for a belief that, he felt, derived from the Gospel of John 14:2, "In my Father's house there are many dwelling places. If it were not so, would I have told you that I go to prepare a place for you?"

---

[104]Scholer, David M., "Martyrdom of Marian and James", *Encyclopedia of Early Christianity, Second Ed.*, Routledge, New York, NY, 2013, pg. 729

[105]Moss, *Myth of Persecution*, pg. 210

[106]Moss, *Myth of Persecution*, pg. 209-210

Matthew O'Neil

Irenaeus felt this meant that there would be mansions for people who were in the upper tier, so it would seem, in the afterlife. People at the top in said mansions were able to see the savior (presumably Jesus), the next layer was "in the heavens," then paradise, and finally "the city" of God. So, much like what the martyrs and those that accepted the views of martyrdom believed, there was a multi-tiered system to reward in paradise.

Some later philosophers and theologians started to revive beliefs that had once been held by the Jewish faith, including those that offered promises of redemption in the afterlife. Among those was Cyprian, the bishop of Carthage and Christian writer in the third century CE. Cyprian not only advanced the idea of being united with Jesus in the afterlife, something people of Irenaeus' mindset would obviously disagree with, but also that humans would rejoin their loved ones.[107] This was a belief that Judaism once held, but was thrown out when new laws prohibiting communication with the dead were implemented.

Lactantius, a Christian writer and the advisor to Emperor Constantine in Rome, held the belief that, when we were brought into heaven, we would be capable of remembering our whole lives.[108] While Lactantius' belief raises some rather interesting questions, like whether we will remember the good *and* the bad, he held some rather thought-provoking views, too. This included the view that, once Rome falls apart (which happened about 200 years after his death), the antichrist would appear and the end of the world would happen.[109] It is

[107]Russell, *A History of Heaven*, pg. 65
[108] Ibid.
[109]Froom, Leroy, *the Prophetic Faith of Our Fathers, Vol. 1*, pg. 356-357, http://docs.adventistarchives.org//doc_info.asp?DocID=42770, retrieved April 21, 2014

interesting because, as we will discover during our time discussing these topics, the authors of the New Testament canon clearly felt that the Roman Empire was the problem, and the empire collapsing, while still marking the end of the age and welcoming in God's kingdom, would not be the start of the end; it would be the end of the end.

Origen, having a very Platonic view of the afterlife, felt that heaven was, in essence, a place of intelligence. It was a place where a "saved" soul, one that followed Christian scripture and the orthodox beliefs of the Church, could understand the order of the universe, of the cosmos, similarly to how God would perceive it. It is, for some, easy to see why Origen's beliefs and views were deemed heretical and heavily questioned during his time.[110]

Augustine, a Christian theologian and philosopher living in the fourth and fifth centuries CE, reportedly had a divine experience that had helped him rediscover what the heavenly life was like. According to his *Confessions*, he and his mother had an experience of "the greatest possible delights of our bodily senses, radiant as they might be with the brightest of corporeal light, could not be compared with the joy of that [eternal] life." Augustine's experience was, to him, a justification of the Platonic philosophy of paradise in the heavens.[111]

When we reach the Middle Ages, we start to get some more defined, specific images of how heaven will appear. Giacomo of Verona, a Franciscan friar who lived in the thirteenth century, composed a poem titled "On the Heavenly Jerusalem". In this poem, he uses imagery from the Book of Revelation to describe the structure of heaven, but there are images of individual

---

[110]Russell, *A History of Heaven*, pg. 76
[111]McDannell and Lang, *Heaven: A History*, pg. 55-56

residences that are not found in scripture. Despite the fact that these details aren't found in the Bible, that is the only source he claims to have called upon for details: "The Holy Writ and all its clauses testify..." And while the poem claims that none of the housing "might be found beneath the sky," it is clear that Giacomo was calling on images of Romanesque buildings and architecture found in the very city in which he lived. A woman named Gerardesca of the Camaldolese order, who lived in the thirteenth century, held a vision of the heavenly kingdom in a very similar way. Both derived from Revelation and their own places of residence —as a home on the outside of a city looking in. Heaven would be a kingdom where all were welcome, none refused or removed, none were hungry or cold. Both are instances of pulling from scripture and the product of their own environment.[112]

Within the Church itself, things are starting to get even more removed from the view of the afterlife pioneered by the Jewish tradition. Thomas Aquinas, a friar, priest, philosopher, and theologian in the thirteenth century, wrote during a council on the Apostle's Creed, "The first point about eternal life is that man is united with God. For God himself is the reward and end of all our labors."[113] So, instead of being separated from God, and unworthy to be in his presence as the Jews held prior to the birth and rise of Christianity, Augustine advocated for a closeness between the believer and God.

---

[112]McDannell and Lang, *Heaven: A History*, pg. 74-76

[113]Aquinas, Thomas, "Article 12: Life Everlasting", *Exposito in Symbolum Apostolorum: the Apostles Creed*, translated by Joseph B. Collins, edited by Joseph Kenny, O. P., New York, NY, 1939, http://dhspriory.org/thomas/Creed.htm#12, retrieved April 21, 2014

Beyond that, during the Renaissance and after, we see works of art like "Souls and the Trinity" by Giovanni di Paolo in the fifteenth century, "the Last Judgment" by Fra Angelico, and "Paradise" by Dieric Bouts envisioning a celestial paradise where the dead join God in heaven. Also in poetry, like Pierre de Ronsard in his ode "O pucelle plus tender," where he writes, "Passing through where raging Pluto reigns/We will arrive on scented plains..."[114]

Even during the Reformation, art like Louys Riche's "Le paradis" and Antonin Politi's "the Blessed Virgin in heaven" show a very densely populated afterlife in the celestial realm. French Bishop Francis de Sales, on All Saints Day in 1617, told the nuns at the Annecy parish that the blessed not only see God, but "hear him talk and themselves talk to him." He did this as an effort, among the efforts of many during this time, to humanize the heavenly realm and make it more accessible to others.[115]

It stands to reason that, given what has been explored and documented up to this point, we now have a solid understanding of how the belief evolved from a complete separation from God to being united with him upon death. To document any further would only prove redundant and, forgive the pun, beating a dead horse.

Conclusion

What started as a mere "land of the dead," borrowing concepts from Greek tradition, thanks to the Hellenization of the Israelites, turned into something much more as time progressed. When Judaism first took on the belief in an afterlife, starting,

---

[114]McDannell and Lang, *Heaven: A History*, pg. 126
[115]McDannell and Lang, *Heaven: A History*, pg. 165

perhaps, around the time of the exile in the sixth century BCE, it was merely a separation from Yahweh —the creator God of their faith. But when they became persecuted, it evolved into a multi-tiered dwelling where the worse you were to God's creation, and people, the further removed you were from him.

It was not until after Christianity was birthed, during its earliest followers' time that a more divine paradise, of sorts, emerged. First starting on earth, as so many of the gospel evangelists and Paul promoted. Again, thanks largely in part to Greek philosophers like Plato and their physics of "up is better than down," the heavens then became the promised, reimagined Israel the people of God were waiting for. And, as time progressed, it became the almost polar opposite of what the belief was, as it originated in Judaism several centuries, even a millennia ago, prior to some changes.

With the changes taking place, most in instances of a change in cultural circumstances, it is easy to see why scripture is truly a product of the environment in which it was created. We also see why, after nearly two millennia of advocacy and championing of these texts, the vision of paradise promised beyond this life, let alone any afterlife, has evolved into what we know it to be today. And if that is the case, we should expect to see such changes, and we shall, as we progress through other areas and avenues dealing with life after death of the body.

Chapter 2: Hell

Hebrew Bible

There is a very interesting fact about the concept of Hell that not many people truly understand or appreciate. When looking through the Bible for the subject of Hell, the Hebrew Bible is completely devoid of any notion of such a place. There are instances in which the notion of "Sheol" is substituted for Hell, but it is not the "fire and brimstone" place of the afterlife that people would come to associate with "Hell" in our modern understanding. In fact, in some translations, Hell is used in place of Sheol 65 times. Even the word Hades, which is the Greek equivalent of the underworld that Judaism adapted into Sheol, is used 26 times in the Apocrypha, and 10 times in the New Testament. Here too, we find Hades, the underworld where all the dead went to, being replaced with Hell.[116]

When Hell is referenced in the Bible, or a word like Sheol is used in its place, it is often in the context of being under God's control. Like in Deuteronomy 32:22, when God states that he can create fire capable of destroying Sheol, "For a fire is kindled by my [God's] anger, and burns to the depths of Sheol...I will heap disasters on them, with venom of things crawling in the dust." Hell is also within his sight, in Psalm 139:8, a Psalm labelled "The Inescapable God." "If I ascend to Heaven, you are

---

[116]Reicke, Bo, "Hell", *the Oxford Guide to the Bible*, Oxford University Press, New York, NY, 1993, pg. 277

there; If I make my bed in Sheol, you are there."[117] Although other writers of the Hebrew Bible intended to show that Sheol was out of God's sight and control, this view sheds some new light on the subject.

While we have already touched upon the concept of Sheol and the underworld in the Hebrew Bible, it would help to understand some of the imagery used with the concept of Sheol so we are able to differentiate between the modern understanding of Hell and how it derived from misinterpretations of the text. As a prime example, Psalm 106:16-18 reads, "The earth opened up and swallowed up Dathan...fire also broke out in their company; the flame burned up their wicked." This comes from the Book of Numbers 16:30-35, where Dathan and a group of 250 others are offering praise to an idol. The narrative states that "Sheol" opened up and "swallowed" the group, and "fire came out from the LORD and consumed the 250 men..." At first glance, it would appear that the fire would be what we would associate with Hell, or the realm of the afterlife we assume is where sinners would be punished. However, we must notice that it states at Numbers 16:35 that the fire comes *from* Yahweh, not Sheol. It is, in fact, completely separate from Sheol.[118]

Isaiah 14:9-15 also offers some imagery that we might, today, connect with the concept of Hell — including the notion that "maggots are the bed beneath you, and worms are your covering." There are even statements that suggest Satan said he would "ascend to heaven" and raise his "throne above the star

---

[117]Reicke. *Oxford Guide*, pg. 278
[118]Hackett, Jo Ann, "Numbers", *the Harper Collins Study Bible*, HarperOne, New York, NY, 1993, pg. 225

of God..." only to be "brought down...to the depths of the Pit." But if we look at the passage in its entirety, we see that Sheol is used as the name of the location; we must remember that the title "the Pit" was synonymous with Sheol. We also need to understand the context — Isaiah was written during the Babylonian exile and this passage refers to, or is directed at, the Babylonian king. This is similar to how Ezekiel made a statement to the king of Tyrus in chapter 28. It also makes sense that, in light of being in captivity in Babylon (which was included in the Mesopotamian Empire), Isaiah uses imagery from *the Epic of Gilgamesh*, a Babylonian myth. On Tablet VII, Enkidu, a central character to the story, warns Gilgamesh of a dream he had where he was dragged down to the netherworld. However, the netherworld did not equate to Hell; it was just the residence of all the dead.[119]

Again, in Isaiah 26:14, we see more references to what would become Hell: "The dead do not live; shades do not rise - because you have punished and destroyed them, and wiped out all memory of them." It seems rather dark and dreary, but if you continue on a verse or so later, you see the author make mention of spreading the borders of Israel. This is because, instead of Hell, this passage is in reference to the destruction of the Persian antagonists to the Israelites. Because the Israelites thought God had vanquished, or helped them vanquish, the enemy that was the Persians, the people of Israel could now expand their borders and make the land promised to them, as the Pentateuch stated, even larger. As in many other cases, this was not about the next world and punishment in the hereafter, it was about the present world and the blessing that the Israelites felt was

---

[119]Turner, *the History of Hell*, pg. 41

Matthew O'Neil

brought upon them. [120] So, while this could have been in reference to punishment after death, these passages were more than likely meant to demonstrate that the Israelites believed an untimely death was brought on by wicked behavior.[121]

Post-exilic Jews retained the concept of the underworld, but kept it provisional. We will get to the reason for this in a later section (as it involves the belief in resurrection), but this helps us to understand why we start to see a belief in, if not complete annihilation, of why the wicked go to the underworld. In Psalm 9:17, as an example, the author writes, "The wicked shall depart to Sheol, all the nations that forget God." Or at Psalm 31:17, "let the wicked be put to shame; let them go dumbfounded to Sheol." Or even Psalm 55:15, "let [my enemies] go down alive to Sheol; for evil is in their homes and in their hearts." Even Isaiah writes, at 5:14, "Sheol has enlarged its appetite and opened its mouth beyond measure..." and at 28:18, "your covenant with death will be annulled, and your agreement with Sheol will not stand...you will be beaten down by it." These sections make no mention of Sheol being a place of torment, but instead it is an instance of the wicked deserving death.[122] We will see this same motif repeated in the writings of Paul.

This is not to say that a concept of punishment in the afterlife was completely absent from Judaism, but it is certainly absent from the canonized books of the Hebrew Bible. Even the apocrypha, which the Catholic faith accepts as books that are relevant "historical" documents of the faith prior to Jesus of Nazareth's ministry, lack concepts similar to Hell. However, in a

[120]Turner, *the History of Hell*, pg. 42
[121]Reicke, *Oxford Guide*, pg. 278
[122]Ibid.

non-canonical Jewish book, written after the exile in Babylon between 300 and 100 BCE, there are concepts of, not punishment, but separateness in Sheol. The book, called 1 Enoch, says at 22:10-11, "And in the same way likewise are sinners separated when they die, and are buried in the earth; judgment not overtaking them in their lifetime." So, even in later instances of the Jewish faith, though not part of scripture, there is still a belief, or a desire, for separate realms for those who have sinned against Yahweh and his chosen people.[123]

Punishment, as noted, was certainly given in the afterlife, even if one had received punishment in his or her own lifetime, as Job would suggest. However, extra-biblical texts, like those in *Erubin* 41B, *Shabbat* 33B, and *Rosh Ha-Shanah* 17A, stated that the punishment was for no more than twelve months, as Gehenna, a flaming pit on the outskirts of Jerusalem which bled into the mythology of the afterlife, was viewed not only as a place of punishment, but of purification. The *Pesikta Rabbati* (53:2) dictates that, once a sinner's punishment was received, they were forgiven from all iniquities. Exceptions were made for heretics, adulterers (men who committed adultery with married women), and those who did not believe the words of the Torah. Those people were sentenced for longer. Comparatively, if we look at sources like Erubin 19A, even when a sinner was at Gehenna's gate, it was still possible for that person to repent before Yahweh. Or, if that person had had a life filled with suffering, they could avoid Gehenna all together, as is noted in Erubin 41B. [124] So, a person could not only have a limited sentence, but could avoid one altogether, as is noted in these texts. It is easy to say some were committed to their sentence for

---

[123]Reicke, *Oxford Guide*, pg. 277
[124]Raphael, *Jewish Views*, pg. 144

eternity, but that is not the case, and it is something we will return to when we talk about "eternity" in the next section.

1 Enoch also demonstrates the later development of the multi-tiered Sheol, where the wicked are pushed out to be further separated from God. At 22:1-14, Enoch is speaking with an angel named Raphael. They hear a voice shouting out to the heavens, only to discover that it is Abel, of Cain and Abel. Raphael then tells Enoch that there are separate spaces for the deceased, though they all gather in the underworld. "And in the same way likewise are sinners separated when they die...Thus has there existed a separation between the souls of those who utter complaints, and of those who watch for their destruction, to slaughter them in the day of sinners." Sinners were still punished; they were cursed to a flaming gorge called Gehenna. [125] It is not Hell, and it is not even part of the underworld. But, we shall return to this concept in just a little bit.

New Testament

If we turn to the earliest writings of the New Testament, those of Paul of Tarsus, what do we find about a place of suffering? Well, honestly, we find next to nothing. Paul never once mentions Hell or anything indicative of a place of suffering and punishment. He does state that those chosen first to be brought into God's kingdom will escape the final judgment at the end of the age.[126] Paul does also mention, on three separate occasions, those not brought into the kingdom of God. One is at 1

[125] Reicke, *Oxford Guide*, pg. 278
[126] Tabor, James, *Paul and Jesus: How the Apostle Transformed Christianity*, Simon and Schuster, New York, NY, 2012, pg. 125

Corinthians 6:9-10, then at Galatians 5:19-21, and Ephesians 5:5. In these passages, Paul writes that, among others, idolaters, adulterers, thieves, the greedy, the sexually immoral, and those participating in witchcraft will not be welcomed into God's kingdom. However, he does not say where they will go if they are not being brought into the kingdom of God. He does write what happens to them though, at Romans 5:12, when speaking about Jesus offering himself for the sins of humanity through Adam. Paul writes that "death came through sin." So, in so many words, death is the punishment given to those who sin. We all sin, according to Paul, and so we all die. This concept would later become a belief held by the Anglican Church called "annihilation theory" or "annihilationism." The belief is that, unless someone is welcomed into the kingdom of God, they would be destroyed rather than suffer eternal punishment.[127]

In terms of later writings, the gospel accounts do not offer us much insight into the world of everlasting punishment. Mark, the earliest of the four gospels, has only one passage that references a place sounding like Hell. At Mark 9:43-48, it says, "If your hand causes you to stumble, cut it off; it is better for you to enter life maimed than to have two hands and to go to hell, to the unquenchable fire." It seems straightforward, yes? Here is our first indication of the land of eternal punishment called "Hell"! However, this is not the case.

"Hell," in this instance, is actually replacing the Greek word *Gehenna*. This word refers to the valley of the son of Hinnom, which we see in 2 Kings 23:10 in reference to Ben-hinnom, where people were punished by being thrown into a valley of

---

[127]Turner, Alice K., *the History of Hell*, Harcourt Brace and Company, New York, NY, 1993, pg. 52

fire.[128] We also see mention of this in Jeremiah 7:31; again, referenced as the Valley of Hinnom (*ge-hinnom* in Hebrew). It was located in the valleys to the south and west of Jerusalem where garbage, child sacrifice, burning of the deceased, animals, and punishment for the wicked took place. Some of these actions were for the sake of sanitation, and others were for the sake of punishment.[129] These practices were also carried out by Israel's king, as seen in Deuteronomy 18:10 and 2 Kings 16:3. The word affiliated with Gehenna, *Topeth*, also means "burning place," and is mentioned in Isaiah 30:33.[130]

Between the synoptic gospels, Mark, Matthew, and Luke (John makes no mention of a place of punishment in the afterlife or otherwise),[131] and the Epistle of James, there are twelve references that mention a place of torment, and that place is Gehenna, or Gehinnom, like in Matthew 23:33.[132] Even in regards to calling the place of torment Hades, as is seen in Matthew 11:23, Luke 10:15, and Luke 16:23, these correspond to the concept of Gehenna as a place of punishment. Given that Gehenna was known as the valley where punishment was carried out, for the wicked specifically, it seems likely they were not writing about a place of eternal punishment, but of the fiery valley where criminals were punished for their heinous deeds.[133]

In the Gospel of Matthew, written 10 to 15 years after the Gospel of Mark, Gehenna is still an idea used by the author. At

---

[128]Römer, *Oxford Annotated*, pg. 568

[129]Turner, *the History of Hell*, pg. 40

[130]Hutton, Rodney R., "Jeremiah", *the New Oxford Annotated Bible*, Oxford University Press, New York, NY, 2010, pg. 1073

[131]Turner, *the History of Hell*, pg. 53

[132]Turner, *the History of Hell*, pg. 54

[133]Reicke, *Oxford Guide*, pg. 277

5:22, the writer uses "Gehenna," which is replaced with "hell" in later translations, as it is at 23:15 with the warning that "[the Pharisees] make the new convert twice as much a child of Gehenna as yourselves." Similarly, at Matthew 10:28, when the author writes "fear him who can destroy both soul and body in hell." Hell, again, is replacing the Greek "Gehenna". Luke 8:31 uses the word "abyss" to allude to something that might be perceived as hell, but "abyss" was also used in the Hebrew Bible to refer to Sheol, similar to how Matthew 11:23 uses Hades. It is the place of the dead that is under Yahweh's control.[134] Matthew also refers to "the place of destruction" at 7:13, but this, again, is a word used in place of Sheol, and it parallels passages like Proverbs 4:18 and Psalm 1:6, which are nearly identical.

Matthew does seem to implement an idea that we do not see much of anywhere else in the New Testament. This is the concept of "weeping and gnashing of teeth" that people associate with Hell. We see this at 8:12, 13:42, 50, 22:13, 24:51, and 25:30. Luke even uses this idea at 13:28, but if we see how the author of Luke uses this idea in Acts 7:54-60, it makes the concept clear to us. The passage in Acts speaks of the first martyr of Christianity, Stephen. And, when he is about to be put to death, Stephen has noticeably angered the council that is about to stone him. As they listen to him, "they became enraged and ground their teeth at him." Grinding, or gnashing, ones teeth was actually a sign of anger and protest. We see instances of this at Job 16:9, where it is actually God doing the gnashing of teeth. Psalm 35:16 has the author referring to people of this world gnashing teeth at him, and Psalm 37:12, which mentions the wicked gnashing their teeth at the author. But, he writes, "the LORD laughs at the wicked, for he sees that *their day is coming* [emphasis added]."

It appears that this is something not reserved for those in Hell, but it is, instead, an act of protest against someone, whether to mock or show outrage. Even God laughs at them because, although they are not being punished yet, they will be eventually. However, what is never stated in any of these passages is that this gnashing of teeth is done, either in the netherworld, or for an eternity. The flames, as used in several of the "gnashing" passages of Matthew, are likely signs of God's judgment upon sinners; flame inflicted by God, not by a place of eternal punishment.

Matthew 25 also has several important ideas for us to understand in regards to the concept of eternity or infinity in the biblical texts. At 25:41, Matthew writes of an "everlasting fire" that the devil and his angels will be in (and this is similar to the Numbers passage, as well as others in the New Testament including the Epistle to the Hebrews; it is imagery of God's judgment, not flames in Hell), and of "everlasting punishment" at 25:46. "Everlasting" and "eternal" both derive from the same word in Greek; *aeonios.*

It is important for us to understand this word as it helps us comprehend what the original authors meant, because it does not mean what our modern understanding assumes the word means. In our modern world, we understand "eternal," "everlasting," and "infinite" to, more or less, all be synonymous. They are not measures of time, per se, but they represent things that happen non-stop. However, in the Greek world, these were finite concepts with a beginning and an end point. We see these at Romans 16:25 when Paul wrote of "the revelation of the mystery which has been kept secret *for long ages past* [emphasis added]." The part that reads "from long ages past" is actually, in

Greek, the one we have been speaking of, *aeonios*. This same word is also used in 2 Timothy 1:9 and Titus 1:2. Even in the Septuagint, the Greek translation of the Hebrew Bible, the same Greek word is used at Genesis 17:8 and Leviticus 3:17: "This is a lasting ordinance for the generation to come..." While the word may mean a long duration of time, it did not mean an infinite amount of time.[135] This same Greek word is also from where we get our modern word "eon," which has the same exact meaning.

In Luke, when the author uses the story of Lazarus and the rich man at 16:26, it did not indicate the two individuals were separated by Heaven and Hell. Rather, it showed the different realms of the underworld — of Sheol. What we have come to know as hell is actually referred to as "Hades" in Luke 16:23, but it is a separate area in the same underworld that Lazarus is being held in. This is part of the later belief that sinners were housed in separate realms of Sheol — a post exilic belief. The rich man is still capable of communicating with Abraham, which is something he would not be able to do, given the Jewish belief that Sheol was not capable of passing any communication on to the heavenly realm. So, instead of a detail of heaven and hell, the parable of the rich man and Lazarus describes separate areas in the land of the dead.[136]

Outside of the gospels, we do not find any different views when it comes to the underworld and punishment. As an example, in Acts 2:27-31, it reads, "For you will not abandon my soul to Hades...' He was not abandoned to Hades, nor did his flesh experience corruption.'" As before, it is an instance of

---

[135]"Matthew 25:46", *Ellicott's Commentary for English Readers*, 2013, Biblos.com, http://biblehub.com/commentaries/matthew/25-46.htm, retrieved March 4, 2015
[136]Reicke, *Oxford Guide*, pg. 278

using the Greek concept of the underworld that the Jewish faith adapted into Sheol. It is not a place of punishment, but instead the arena where all the dead reside.[137]

In the epistle to the Hebrews 10:27, the author makes a stern warning of "a fearful prospect of judgment, and a fury of fire that will consume the adversaries." This is not a prediction of an eternal punishment in Hell, as it is never brought up in the conversation. Nor is any idea of the underworld in this passage. Instead, what we find is a description of judgment brought on by God — another way of indicating an "annihilation theory" outlook on humanity by the author. Even at Hebrews 12:29, the author describes God as "a consuming fire." So, it is similar to the passage from Numbers with Sheol opening up to consume the group. The fire is not from Sheol, or from Hell in this instance, but is, instead, from the God of the Israelites.[138]

Similarly, in the Epistle of Jude, verse six, the author writes to a community and warns them of angels that have found judgment. This was likely written to a community that sought after something better than what they were being offered through their faith, and the author was warning them in a way that called on concepts taken out of the Sodom and Gomorrah story. While there is no explicit mention of Hell and eternal punishment, negative consequences are suggested. These threats are something along the lines of what happened in Sodom and Gomorrah. In other words, as was dictated in our section about Job and his circumstances, if people were wicked, they received

---

[137] Reicke, *Oxford Guide*, pg. 277

[138] Attridge, Harold W., "Hebrews", *the Oxford Bible Commentary*, Oxford University Press, New York, NY, 2001, pg. 1251

their just rewards in this life — even if that meant being punished with death.[139]

At the end of Jude's epistle, at verses 22 and 23, the author writes, "And have mercy on some who are wavering; save others by snatching them out of the fire..." This is another passage that seemingly refers to saving individuals from the fires of Hell, as we have come to know such warnings from the Christian faith; but, instead, it is a warning of fire that will be sent by God. The author intended the warning to be seen as similar to the punishment of Sodom and Gomorrah, and Korah from the Book of Numbers 16:21 who was enveloped in fire *from* God.[140] A similar instance is seen at 2 Peter 3:7, where the "godless" are destroyed by fire. This ties into Paul's annihilation theory —that the wicked are utterly destroyed in God's judgment. But, what is more, in the same passage the author writes, "the present heaven and earth have been reserved for fire..." While still a part of God's judgment, the fire is not from Hell; it comes from God as he means to destroy, not just the wicked or godless, but all of heaven and earth. We see the same use of fire with God's judgment at Isaiah 66:15, Zephaniah 1:18, and, as we shall see, Revelation 18:8.[141]

When we get to Revelation, we find a concept that is also shared in 2 Peter. This is a new idea that has not been shared in

[139]Rowland, C., "Jude", *the Oxford Bible Commentary*, Oxford University Press, New York, NY, 2001, pg. 1285

[140]Nida, Eugene A., translator, and Rhodes, Erroll F., editor, "Jude", *the Good News Study Bible with Deuterocanonical/Apocrypha*, the American Bible Society, New York, NY, 1993, pg. 1667

[141]Nida, Eugene A., translator, and Rhodes, Erroll F., editor, "the Second Letter from Peter", *the Good news Study Bible with Deuterocanonical/Apocrypha*, the American Bible Society, New York, NY, 1993, pg. 1653

any of the other New Testament writings and, certainly, might lend credence to modern understandings of what Hell may be. In 2 Peter 2:4, the author writes, "For if God did not spare the angels when they sinned, but cast them into Tartarus, and committed them to chains of deepest darkness to be kept until judgment..." First, this is a concept that cries back to the story of the "sons of God" in Genesis 6:2, with the heavenly beings that bring corruption to the earth. Second, this concept of Tartarus, also found in Revelation chapter 20,[142] is not Hell. Instead, this is a Greek concept that was stolen and implemented in the writings of early Jewish-Christians.

In Greek myth, Tartarus was the prison of the Titans.[143] It is where the Cyclops, Hecatonchires, Cronus, and many other Greek deities were housed once the gods of Olympus took control.[144] Plato even makes reference to Tartarus in his work *Gorgias*, saying that the good souls going to the Blessed Isles, while the wicked go to Tartarus.[145] In Revelation 20, the author writes of an angel seizing Satan and locking him in the pit, Tartarus. It seems only fitting that such a figure as Satan is locked in a cell that was conceived as only being capable of holding deities, rather than this being a location for punishment

[142]Ruiz, Jean-Pierre, "Revelation", *the New Oxford Annotated Bible,* Oxford University Press, New York, NY, 2010, pg, 2177
[143]Tiller, Patrick A., "the Second Letter of Peter", *the New Oxford Annotated Bible*, Oxford University Press, New York, NY, 2010, pg. 2134
[144]Hesiod, *the Homeric Hymns and Homerica with an English Translation*, translated by Huge G. Evelyn-White, Harvard University Press, Cambridge, MA, 1914, pg. 820-822 & 868
[145]Jackson, Robin, Lycos, Kimon, and Tarrant, Harold, translators, *Commentary on Plato's Gorgias*, by Olympidorus, Brill Publishers, Leiden, the Netherlands, 1998, pg. 305

for all. Revelation does not even imply that this is a holding for all sinners or wicked persons, but only Satan.

Parallels between the Second Peter account and Revelation 20 are pretty strong. John writes, in Revelation, that the angel descends into the pit with a "great chain." In 2 Peter 2:4, the author dictates that the angels were not spared, but were cast into Tartarus and "committed to chains of deepest darkness to be kept until the judgment..." This also would appear to be the place where the listed dragon, who is "the Devil and Satan" would be placed, as these are seen as being rather dominant, supernatural figures within the text, similar to the deities housed in Tartarus in Greek mythology. And, very much like what is mentioned in 2 Peter, it was expected that the Devil would be kept in Tartarus until "the final eschatological consummation."[146]

Earlier in Revelation there are other mentions of the underworld, but they are similar to how other books reference the abode of the dead. In Revelation 1:18, it says "I have the keys of Death and of Hades." Also in Revelation 6:8, "I looked and there was a pale green horse! Its rider's name was Death, and Hades followed with him..." And at 20:13-14, "Death and Hades gave up the dead that were in them..." In these instances, Death and Hades are not only synonymous, but they also refer simply to the land of the dead, Sheol. This author held a view similar to Paul's: that Jesus, who is the one speaking in the mentioned passage of Revelation, holds the keys to the land of the dead and can overcome death to bring everlasting life.[147] Later in Revelation, in 9:1-11, a star, representing an angel, falls

---

[146]Ruiz, *Oxford Annotated*, pg. 2177
[147]Ruiz, *Oxford Annotated*, pg. 2156

to earth and happens to have the key to "the bottomless pit." The pit, as we will remember again, is another name for Sheol. This angel is even given a name; "...his name in Hebrew is Abaddon..." Once again, this is a word from the Hebrew Bible in reference to Sheol. It is used at Job 26:6 and Proverbs 15:11, and is personified, as it is in Revelation, at Job 28:22.[148]

Historically, the fallen star, or angel, may refer to the Parthians going to war with Rome. There was a period of about 720 years between Rome and the Persians, and the Parthian war took up nearly 300 years of that—from 66 BCE to 217 CE.[149] It is still not Hell as it would be viewed by contemporary Christians.

Now, the one part of Revelation that would seem to imply an eternity of punishment very much like what we understand Hell to be, is in chapter 20, verses 7 through 10, and this also applies to Matthew 25:41. It reads, "And the devil who had deceived them was thrown into the lake of fire and sulfur, where the beast and the false prophet were, and they will be tormented day and night forever and ever." It certainly sounds like the promises of Hell we know today, but that would be without understanding the Jewish roots and context in which this book was written. In verse seven, there is a reference to Gog and Magog where the nations will gather together for battle. This is also something that Revelation makes reference to at 16:14-16 and 19:17-21.[150]

---

[148]Ibid.

[149]Bivar, H.D.H., "the Political History of Iran Under the Arsacids", *the Cambridge History of Iran*, Cambridge University Press, Cambridge, UK, 1968, pg. 57

[150]Ruiz, *Oxford Annotated,* pg. 2177

What is more important is realizing that this is something borrowed from the Book of Ezekiel. In chapters 38 and 39 of Ezekiel, we have the Gog of Magog oracles; they are a part of early apocalyptic literature. [151] And in this section of Ezekiel, specifically 38:22, we see "With pestilence and bloodshed I will enter into judgment with him; and I will pour down torrential rains and hailstones, fire and sulfur, upon him and his troops and the many people that are with him." This part of the Hebrew Bible also implies that there are nations gathered from the outmost parts of the world to attack the people of Israel at the center of the earth, much like the battle that is described in Revelation. Actually, it is nearly an identical copy of the battle described in Ezekiel, inclusive of the enemies of Israel being destroyed by fire. We must acknowledge, however, that the fire is not of the underworld, but comes from God in the heavenly realm. [152]

Satan

What conversation about Hell would be complete without studying its "ruler," Satan! As stated, Satan is believed to be the merciless ruler over this realm. Not only that, he is believed to influence humanity to sin against God, commit atrocious acts, and to just be down-right nasty. Unless one is an evangelical, committed to the concept of God being in charge of natural disasters and the effects have on humankind due to their sin, the faithful might believe these are caused by Satan as well.

---

[151] Cook, Stephen L., "Ezekiel", *the New Oxford Annotated Bible*, Oxford University Press, New York, NY, 2010, pg. 1214

[152] Bauckham, Richard, "Revelation", *the Oxford Bible Commentary*, pg. 1303

What might surprise the faithful is that nothing could be further from the truth when it comes to Satan and his alleged role in the afterlife and the present one, too. Starting in the Hebrew Bible, Satan is not a name, but a title. We see the character in the familiar story of Job, chapter one. In this story, a character called *the* satan, or the accuser, joins heavenly beings, called "sons of God" (*bene 'elohim* in Hebrew), to "present themselves before the Lord" (Job 1:6). This is actually a divine council, which has parallel references in 1 Kings 22:19-22, and Psalm 82:1. We meet the satan, from the Hebrew *ha-satan*, who is an adversary of Job, not God, as he is of other humans in Zechariah 3:1. The Greeks translated this as *diabolos*, meaning "one who throws something across one's path."[153] Instead, the satan acts as a part of God's council on earth. His purpose, in this story, is to question Job's obedience to God; it stands to reason that it would be questionable whether Job glorifies God out of love or for high standing and gifts received from God.[154]

Job specifically has the satan tell God, upon his request, that he has travelled "to and fro on the earth, and from walking up and down it." He says this because, as a member of the divine council, the satan was Yahweh's "eyes and ears" on the earth. In Hebrew, *stn* sounds incredibly close to *shut*, which means "to roam," adding, perhaps, to the idea of a roaming eye of God.[155] What is more, this also bears a striking resemblance to the Persian secret police that existed during the sixth century BCE under King Darius, who had established a Persian complex in

---

[153]Pagels, Elaine, *the Origin of Satan: How Christians Demonized Jews, Pagans, and Heretics*, Vintage Books, New York, NY, 1996, pg. 39
[154]Clines, David J.A., "Job", *the New Oxford Annotated Bible*, Oxford University Press, New York, NY, 2010, pg. 727
[155]Pagels, *the Origin of Satan*, pg. 41

Judah. They roamed the land looking for any signs of disloyalty to the King and were known as "the King's eyes and ears."[156]

There is also an extra-biblical reference to the satan in a somewhat similar story. In the Book of Jubilees, an ancient Jewish text dating to the first century BCE, there is an angel known as Mastema that takes on the same role that the satan does in Job. He tells God that Abraham loves his son, Isaac, so why not test him to see if he will follow through with his faith? He has God test Abraham's faith by commanding him to sacrifice his son. This leads to Abraham praying to God not to let evil spirits lead him astray in his mission to sacrifice Isaac.[157]

In the Hebrew Bible, sometimes God, or angels that were God's representative on earth, were called "the satan," or adversary. In Numbers 22:22-32, the story of the talking donkey, it reads, "God's anger was kindled because he was going, and the angel of the LORD took his stand in the road as his adversary (*stn*)." So, not only is the satan a member of the divine council, as we see in Job and Zechariah, but also representative of Yahweh himself.

But the satan was not always imagined as a divine figure. In 1 Samuel 29:3-4, we learn of the Philistines being bothered by David, before he became king. The Philistines insisted on sending David away as a result. "Send the man [David] back...or else he may become an adversary [*stn*] to us in the battle." We have a divine figure, then Yahweh, and now King David, who is said to be the one responsible for bringing the Israelites' Messiah through his blood line, all being labelled as the

---

[156]Sinclair, May, *Infamous Eve: A History*, Wheatmark, Inc., Tucson, AZ, 2007, pg. 67
[157]Pagels, *the Origin of Satan*, pg. 54

adversary, the satan, in the Hebrew Bible. It seems rather obvious that the times in which *stn* or *ha-satan* are used in Hebrew scripture are not referring to a specific individual, let alone someone working against God.

There's also an earthly satan in 2 Samuel 19, though it is not David this time. Instead, David is confronting someone that fought against him and was now asking for forgiveness —the sons of Zeruiah. At verse 22, David says, "What have I to do with you, you sons of Zeruiah, that you should today become *an adversary* to me?" Because David's nephew Abishai, a member of the royal court, views the disrespectful behavior of the sons of Zeruiah as warranting a death penalty, what David is doing is actually using legal terms of accusation. Abishai works as one that would lay out the accusation, but David would be the one determining the punishment. Ergo, David opts to let them live, all while using legal terminology to let them know that a capital offense had taken place.[158] So now we are finding that "satan" was used not only as one who was an adversary, but it was also a legal term used for allegations of treason in courts.

In 1 Chronicles 21:1, the author references "the adversary", and how this adversary came into the royal house of David leading to sin. However, after David excludes the population of a rather small group of people, the tribes of Levi and Benjamin, God is displeased. But David says, at verse eight, "I have sinned greatly in that I have done this thing...I have done very foolishly." David, in essence, takes responsibility for his actions. Similarly to Job, there is then a group of angels that work against David and Israel, bringing God's vengeance upon them and

---

[158]Wray, T.J., and Mobley, Gregory, *the Birth of Satan: Tracing the Devil's Biblical Roots*, Palgrave Macmillan, New York, NY, 2005, pg. 54

killing 70,000 Israelites with a plague. It appears there was an angel that was part of a council, that worked against David, not against God. This adversary is another cry back to the story of Job and, it is clear, is not an opponent of God as later story tellers would adapt the figure of Satan to become.[159]

In 1 Kings 11:14, we see another instance of an adversary, or satan, being sent *by God* for a purpose—namely to cause trouble for King Solomon. "Then the LORD raised up an adversary [satan] against Solomon, Hadad the Edomite; he was of the royal house of Edom." A few verses later, at 11:23, another satan is sent to bother Solomon: "God raised up another adversary against Solomon, Rezon son of Eliad, who had fled from his master, King Hadadezer of Zobah." So, not only is the satan an earthly being, or two in this instance, but they are controlled by God, himself. This whole concept of Satan being in opposition to God is starting to sound questionable.

Outside of biblical writings, a court historian, writing around the same time that Job was written (550 BCE), described "the satan" as being responsible for influencing King David, nearly five centuries before, to initiate a census for tax purposes. This was something that was viewed so negatively that even David's own military let it be known that they were opposed to carrying out David's orders, nearly starting a military uprising against the king. However, after David pushed back and let them know he was serious about the census and taxation, the military eventually gave in.[160]

---

[159]Pagel, *the Origin of Satan*, pg. 42
[160]Bloom, Harold, *Satan*, Infobase Publishing, New York, NY, 2009, pg. 199

Now, it should be made clear, the snake in the Eden story in Genesis is not, in fact, Satan, or the devil. Nowhere in the Genesis account does it make any sort of recognition of the snake as Satan, or even a satan. It was not until later centuries that the snake was equated with the devil. In *The Life of Adam and Eve*, a retelling of the creation account written in the first century CE, Eve says, "The devil answered me through the mouth of the serpent."[161] However, even in Revelation the devil is called "the serpent" at 12:9 and 20:2, so it is easy to see why, in contemporary society, people assume the snake was Satan. Other similar characters, taking on paralleled stories and characteristics, include Semyaz in 1 Enoch 6:3 and Belial at Qumran in the Zadokite Document 4:13.[162]

When we arrive at the New Testament, we finally see a single figure personified as the nemesis of God. Satan, or *satanas* in Greek, was also called Beelzebub (the prince of demons) in Matthew 12:24, the tempter in Matthew 4:3, Beliar in 2 Corinthians 6:15, the evil one in 1 John 5:18, and Apollyon in Revelation 9:11. I should point out that, in Revelation 9:11, Apollyon is actually the Greek version of "Abaddon," which is another name for "the pit," which we discussed in our section on Sheol. Lucifer, another familiar name associated with Satan or the devil, was not popularized until the Middle Ages, when the passage Isaiah 14:12-15, "How you have fallen from heaven, day star," used *lucifer*, which translates to "light bearer" in the Latin Vulgate, and is here translated as "day star."[163]

[161]Wray and Mobley, *the Birth of Satan*, pg. 70
[162]Avalos, Hector Ignacio, "Satan", *the Oxford Guide to the Bible*, Oxford University Press, New York, NY, 1993, pg. 679
[163]Pagels, *the Origin of Satan*, pg. 48

The portion of Matthew 4 involving Satan is the familiar story of Jesus in the desert being tempted by Satan. Matthew has already made strong attempts to show Jesus to be the new Moses, creating a parallel account of the slaughter of the male children of Israel with the massacre of the innocent during the nativity story. The account of Jesus in the desert mirrors Moses' fast of 40 days and 40 nights in Exodus 24:18, as well as the pilgrimage through the desert for 40 years. Because Jesus' revelation happens on top of a mountain, where Satan has led him, it also mirrors the story of Moses on top of Mount Pisgah, using the language of Deuteronomy 34:1 and 4. So, while Satan is used to tempt Jesus, he acts as a literary figure, similar to the Beloved Disciple in the Gospel of John, in order to promote Jesus as larger than life—the return of Moses.[164]

The 2 Corinthians passage, referring to Satan as "Beliar," is actually believed to be a later addition to the text, placed there by the Qumran community, given the dualism and vocabulary.[165] This is most noticeable when compared to 2:11, where the Hebrew name, Satan, is used in reference to the character as "the accuser" or "adversary". It is used similarly at 11:14 and 12:7. Satan is also, elsewhere in 2 Corinthians, called "serpent" at 11:3 and "the god of this world" at 4:4. Paul appears to have simply taken the vague character of Satan, seen in stories like Numbers and Job, and added a bit more depth to the story.

In John's gospel, it is important to make note of the perception of the devil, as this particular book paved the road to unprecedented anti-Semitism that still exists today. John took

---

[164] Allison, *Bible Commentary*, pg. 851
[165] MacDonald, Margaret, "2 Corinthians", *the Oxford Bible Commentary*, Oxford University Press, New York, NY, 2001, pg. 1142

actions, previously attributed to Satan in other passages, and applied it to the Jews in his narrative. Very blatantly, in 8:44, the Jews tell Jesus that Abraham is their father, but Jesus claims that, were they Abraham's children, they would act like him and not try and kill him: "You are from your father, the devil, and you choose to do your father's desires." Similarly in 14:30-31, "for the ruler of this world is coming." This is the same "ruler of this world" as seen in the aforementioned passage in John, and in 12:31. When this was written, it was not meant to be inclusive of all Jews, simply the ones that did not follow the Jesus cult. Similarly, Satan was not meant to be affiliated with the Jews, but was meant to show and be synonymous with the opposition that followers of Jesus were met with. [166] So, again, we find a character, or characters, who were meant to demonstrate and push a particular agenda, but were not necessarily conceived as literal figures during the times they were written about.

To piggyback off of the narrative in John, the First Letter of John also refers to those, deceived by sin, to be children of the devil. Given how closely related the two are, using very similar language, imagery, and even the concept of Jews—who do not acknowledge Jesus as the Messiah—as being defectors of, or hostile towards, the faith, it is easy to assume that both the authors of John's gospel, and the epistle of John, likely wrote about very similar figures.[167] And, while it certainly creates an image of a single individual that acts as the adversary of God, or even of Jesus, it does not do much to flesh out the character that people know Satan to be today.

---

[166] Pagels, *the Origin of Satan*, pg. 102, 104-105
[167] Perkins, Pheme, "the First Letter of John", *the New Oxford Annotated Bible*, Oxford University Press, New York, NY, 2010, pg. 2137

A story I grew up hearing and believing was in the Bible, is the story of Satan being cast out of heaven with his angels. However, this is not biblical; instead, it comes from the extra-biblical 2 Enoch (18:3, 29:3): "Here Satanil was hurled from the height together with his angels."[168] "And one from out of the order of angels, having turned away with the order that was under him, conceived an impossible thought, to place his throne higher than the clouds above the earth, that he might become equal in rank to my power."

Revelation is one of the areas into which we must delve the deepest in order to find images of Satan. Revelation lists certain areas as "the throne of Satan" (2: 13), which referred to Pergamum, the center of the imperial cult and one of the first cities to erect a temple dedicated to Rome and Augustus. This is typical for the first 11 chapters of Revelation, where Satan is used to refer to enemies of the Christian communities that existed during the writing of Revelation.[169]

After those chapters, we are then met by the dragon of Revelation 12:9, "that ancient serpent, who is called the Devil and Satan, the deceiver of the whole world". Here, the dragon is likely a representation of the Roman empire, along with the emperors. Like in 13:3, the "death-blow" on one of the heads of the beast likely refers to Julius Caesar. The dragon was representative of the persecution early Christians felt under Roman rule, and the author invoked imagery from the Book of Daniel, with the beast coming from the water, and used references from Job and the character of the accuser, or Satan.

---

[168]Anderson, Gary A., and Stone, Michael E., editors, *Literature on Adam and Eve: Collected Essays*, Brill Academic Publishing, 2000, pg. 64
[169]Wray and Mobley, *the Birth of Satan*, pg. 140-142

Michael, who also helps the people of Israel when the beast of Daniel attacks, is here to save the day in heaven against the serpent.[170] It is clear that, not only does the author know quite a bit about the Hebrew Bible, but he shifts it for his purposes, and the purposes of the churches to which he is writing in order to find allegiance with other followers of Jesus.

Revelation 20 also makes mention of Satan, but it is as a conclusion to all the suffering that the people of Israel, specifically the people who are now followers of Jesus, have been through. In the beginning of Revelation, it states, "The revelation of Jesus Christ, which God gave him to show his servants *what must soon take place* [Emphasis my own]." So, it is predicted, there will be a victory over the Roman Empire. It is said that the empire was causing such torment among the Jews and followers of Jesus, so the kingdom of God should then be given to the righteous—taken away from the Romans.[171]

What is most noticeable in the New Testament, whether it is on a smaller scale like the devil offering temptation, or on a larger scale such as an outright war against the armies of the heavens, Satan is never victorious. Jesus is capable of exorcising the demons that, allegedly, work for Satan, and he silences them. Jesus also resists the temptation of the devil, and labels the Jews, or those who are not faithful to Jesus, as children of the devil. Though they kill him, he still is victorious over death, or so Paul says (Romans 6:9). Some of the epistles speak of those fighting against the followers of Jesus as Satan, or being related to the devil, yet they are not victorious in stopping the first Christians from worshipping. Even in Revelation, try as he, or it, may, the

[170]Ruiz, *Oxford Annotated*, pg. 2168-2169
[171]Bauckham, *Bible Commentary*, pg. 1303

devil is absolutely unsuccessful in holding any sort of power over the figures and groups we read about.

So the question, then, is where does our fear of Satan come from? He is alleged to rule over the wicked, over sinners, in Hell, but we are seeing no sign of Hell, and certainly not an individual capable of commandeering such a place. And, it is funny to mention, *nowhere in the Bible does it say that Satan is the ruler of Hell.* If we are to suspend disbelief, and accept that Satan is alleged to have ruled Hell, then how can we say that he was thrown into "the pit" in Revelation 20:3? He was also locked away in there. Was this the start of in-house arrest?

Outside of the Bible, we need to take into account the story in 1 Enoch, which was written in the third century BCE with some later additions. In this story, the author tells of the birth of Satan and how he and his rebellious angels were cast out of heaven. This story, as it just so happens, is a retelling of the story of the Titans, in Greek mythology, rebelling against Zeus. This actually makes its way into Luke 10:18: "He said to them, 'I watched Satan fall from heaven like a flash of lightning.'"[172] This same story is also found in John 12:31 and Revelation 12:7-12.

Satan is also found in the Qumran literature, written by the Essenes in the first century BCE. This figure not only commanded a "legion," like what is alluded to in Mark's gospel (5:9), on earth, but in heaven as well. The Essenes also felt that the occupation of Palestine served as sufficient evidence of Satan's existence and control of God's chosen people.[173] This is an absolutely distinct example of dualist belief that, incidentally,

---

[172]White, L. Michael, *Scripting Jesus: The Gospels in Rewrite*, Harper One, New York, NY, 2011, pg. 62, iBooks Edition
[173]Wray and Mobley, *the Birth of Satan*, pg. 105

came from Palestinians as well as the Greeks—such as the *Theogony* by Hesiod, involving myths about Uranus, Cronus, and Zeus, among others, and dating to sometime in the eighth to seventh century BCE.[174]

After the Bible

Looking over what is said about Hell in the Hebrew and Christian scriptures, it is hard to understand how the idea of punishment for an eternity really became a "thing." However, if we take a look at post-biblical writings and the early Church fathers and their interpretations, it starts to become much clearer.

"The Apocalypse of Peter," a non-canonical book that would be in the same genre as the Book of Revelation, is one of our earliest writings that gives any indication of beliefs in eternal punishment in the afterlife. This was, in so many words, the precursor to Dante's *Inferno*. In this narrative, we are met with stories of blasphemers who are hung by their tongues over flames. Women who braided their hair to seduce men are also hung over flames by their hair. There are even men hung by their genitals over flames who cried out, "We didn't know it would come to this!"[175]

The Apocalypse of Peter was written in the second century, CE. It was considered, for a time, to be part of the Muratorian

---

[174]Bianchi, Ugo, "Dualism", *the Encyclopaedia Brittanica*, retrieved April 20, 2015,
http://www.britannica.com/EBchecked/topic/172631/dualism/38187/Greece-and-the-Hellenistic-world
[175]Ehrman, Bart, *Forged: Writing in the Name of God - Why the Bible's Authors are Not Who We Think They Are*, Harper One, New York, NY, 2011, pg. 64-65

canon, until a document, now called the "Muratorian fragment," dated to 170 CE, stated that "the Apocalypse of Peter" would no longer be read in the Church. This same canon, however, did not include the books of Hebrews, James, First or Second Peter, or the Third Epistle of John; nor did they include the Wisdom of Solomon.[176]

Second Enoch is another interesting text when it comes to understanding the later traditions behind Hell. This book was likely written during the first century CE, probably before the destruction of the second Temple of Jerusalem, as it commands Jewish followers to still visit the Temple three times a day and makes no mention of it being destroyed. Though it was written prior to the composition of the gospels, it demonstrates a concept of a torturous afterlife. In the narrative, Yahweh shows Enoch the "ten heavens," and the third contains both Paradise and Hell. It is described as a terrible place full of torture; there is darkness, a fiery river, and frost and ice everywhere with merciless angels using sharp weapons to torture the inhabitants. Enoch is told that anyone who breaks the Ten Commandments, is greedy, abuses children, or utilizes magic of any kind, is brought to this area. Performing good deeds, or studying the Torah could help someone escape Gehenna, according to *Pesikta Rabbati.*[177] Even better was that, should someone feel repentant at the gates of Gehenna, they could appeal to God and be granted clemency.[178]

---

[176]Ehrman, Bart, *the New Testament: A Historical Introduction to the Early Christian Writings*, Fourth Edition, Oxford University Press, New York, NY, 2007, pg. 483-485
[177]Turner, *the History of Hell*, pg. 44
[178]Raphael, *Jewish Views*, pg. 144

Parts of the Oral Torah, the Hebrew teachings that were not in the written Torah, also include bits about Gehenna. These were not written down until after the destruction of the Jewish Temple in 70 CE, hence the name "Oral" Torah, and it is hard to distinguish when, exactly, these concepts originated. However, there are parts, like in *Yoma* 89A, that state Gehenna will offer punishment for things like a teacher causing a community to sin.[179]

We do know that some early members of the faith also spoke about something sounding like Hell. Ignatius of Antioch, who was born right after the death of Jesus and died (presumably a martyr's death) in the early second century CE, wrote an epistle titled, "Letter to the Ephesians." In it, at 16:1-2, he writes that anyone who corrupts families and takes them away from Jesus "will depart into unquenchable fire; and so will anyone who listens to him." Ignatius never mentions a place like Hell, Sheol, Hades, Tartarus, or even Gehenna. However, because of where he lived, Syria, its location in relation to Jerusalem, approximately 302 miles (486 kilometers) away, and the close relation he, by tradition, may have had with the earliest followers of Jesus, it seems likely he would have shared a lot of the same views and beliefs, inclusive of punishment in Gehenna.[180]

Augustine of Hippo, a Church father who lived during the fourth and fifth century CE, wrote in his book, *City of God* (20:16), "It is my opinion that the nature of hell-fire and the location of hell are known to no man unless the Holy Ghost

---

[179]Raphael, *Jewish Views*, pg. 142
[180]Peoples, Glenn Andrew, "History of Hell|Hell Before Augustine", *Afterlife*, May 20, 2013, retrieved March 11, 2015, http://www.afterlife.co.nz/2013/theology/history-of-hell/

made it known to him through divine revelation." It is interesting that, after writing this, Augustine then wrote in his book of retractions (Book 2, xxiv) that Hell was located within the earth. About a century after Augustine, Gregory the Great, or Pope Gregory I, wrote in his book *Dialogues* (IV, xlii) that "Some thought Hell is somewhere on earth, others believe it is under the earth." However, John Chrysostom, who lived during the fourth and fifth centuries, CE, said, "We must not ask where Hell is, but how we are to escape it."[181]

Thanks, in part, to the Athanasian Creed, used since the sixth century CE, the problem with exaggerating and stating a biblical position that is not actually in the Bible has been exacerbated. This comes from the part of the creed that states, "They that have done good shall go into everlasting life, and they that have done evil into everlasting fire." This was, in turn, used in later documents created in the Council of Florence and the Second Council of Lyon, between the thirteenth and fifteenth centuries CE. In the Decree of Union, from the Council of Florence, it says, "the souls of those who depart in mortal sin, or only in original sin, go down immediately into hell, to be visited, however, with unequal punishment."[182]

There are also later texts, like the *Gospel of Nicodemus*, dated to the Middle Ages, and a second century text called *Acta Pilati*, or the *Acts of Pilate*, that develop the concepts of Hell. In it is a description similar to Dante Aligheri's *Divine Comedy*, except it describes a tour of Hell as seen by Jesus after his crucifixion. This had a huge influence on medieval views of Hell and the

---

[181]Hontheim, J., "Hell", *the Catholic Encyclopedia*, Robert Appleton Company, New York, NY, 1910, retrieved March 11, 2015, http://www.newadvent.org/cathen/07207a.htm

[182]Ibid.

afterlife, and firmly helped to establish the view of Jesus collecting the righteous from Hell after his execution.[183]

Doctrinal concepts of Hell also came about thanks, in large part, to artistic depictions of the afterlife. As an example, Dante Aligheri's *The Divine Comedy* is a series that follows the protagonist, Dante, being led through the multiple points of the afterlife, including Heaven, Purgatory, and Hell. Prior to Aligheri's book, the dominant belief of punishment in the afterlife was one of purification after a length of suffering. But *The Divine Comedy* opened new possibilities of *contrapassio*, meaning "to suffer the opposite"—eternal suffering, in other words. This meant that a person's soul would suffer a fate in light of, or contrary to, the sin the individual committed whilst still alive. Similarly, people in Purgatory, as described in *Purgatorio* of the same series, suffered as part of their contrition before being allowed to leave and enter the heavenly realm.[184]

When we explore Satan after the Bible, we start to see a trend that had emerged thanks, for the majority of the stretch in belief, to Revelation. Rival groups, or people who challenged or punished the followers of Jesus, became affiliated with Satan. Some of this is even reflected in the gospels, where Mark challenges the powers of evil, or "scribes," like the Pharisees and Herodians. Matthew also demonizes the Pharisees, calling them "sons of hell," saying that those who deny Jesus and his

---

[183]Reid, George, "Acta Pilati", *the Catholic Encyclopedia*, Robert Appleton Co., New York, NY, 1907, retrieved April 22, 2014, http://www.newadvent.org/cathen/01111b.htm

[184]Musa, Mark, *the Divine Comedy Commentary. Volume 1: Inferno*, Penguin Classics, New York, New York, 1984, pages 37-38

movement would be cast into the fires "reserved for the devil and all his angels."[185]

Even in John, the only time we really see Satan is when Judas is possessed by him. Keep in mind, though, that John certainly had an axe to grind. He undermined Peter by having the Beloved Disciple be closest to Jesus at the last supper, get to the tomb first, *believe* that Jesus had been resurrected, and even recognize Jesus after the resurrection before Peter. John makes it a point, prior to Judas' possession, to only give Judas the Eucharist as some backhanded entry against the practice, or perhaps even against Paul who alleges that Jesus, not one of the disciples, had taught him that in a vision. [186] So, we must acknowledge, John sought more to demonize (pardon the expression) groups that believed or felt differently than the church he, and the several others likely to have penned the gospel with him, believed in. Outside of that, we know Justin Martyr, in the second century CE, was baptized, denouncing and rejecting Satan three times, and "realized" that the Pagan gods he had grown up with, and saw others worship, were actually demonic servants of Satan. "We pity those who believe such things," he writes, "for which we know that the *daimones* [Greek; demons] are responsible."[187]

Tatian, another early Christian from the second century CE, postulated that *daimones* had "shown humans a map of the position of the stars, invented destiny - an enormous injustice! ...every human birth is regarded as a kind of theatrical entertainment by those beings of whom Homer says 'among the

---

[185]Pagels, *Origin of Satan*, pg. 110-111

[186]Meier, John, "the Eucharist and the Last Supper: Did it Happen?", *Theology Digest 42*, Winter 1995, pg. 347

[187]Pagels, *the Origin of Satan*, pg. 121-122

gods arouse unquenchable laughter.'" He later added, "We do not follow the guidance of destiny; rather, we reject those demons who established it."[188] This sort of view makes perfect sense, since first, Babylonians were a culture that believed in astrology and its link with destiny,[189] as did the Greeks and Romans. That idea, thanks to Hellenization and Alexander the Great, reached the Persians, Syrians, and central Asia,[190] and then the Islamic world became one affiliated with astrology as well. So not only do we see a faith tainted by astrology in the past, with the Babylonian exile, and in the present day of Tatian, but it also laid the ground work for anti-Islam sentiment for future followers of the faith.

Church father Origen, who lived between the end of the second and beginning of the third centuries CE, also took the approach of identifying enemies and overlords with the devil. In a reply he made to Celsus, a Plato-centered philosopher who had claimed the Christians' insistence to not follow directives was an attempt to dismantle the empire of Rome, Origen wrote, "It is not irrational to form associations contrary to the existing laws...by the devil, form associations contrary to the devil's laws, against his power, to protect those whom they succeed in persuading to revolt against a government which is barbaric and despotic."[191]

Even individuals, who were viewed as "heretics," or those fighting against dogmatic belief in the Christian faith, were

[188]Pagels, *the Origin of Satan*, pg. 133
[189]Barton, Tamsyn, *Ancient Astrology*, Routledge, New York, NY, 1994, pg. 24
[190]Campion, Nicholas, *A History of Western Astrology, Vol. 1: the Ancient World*, Continuum Books, London, UK, 2008, pg. 173
[191]Pagels, *the Origin of Satan*, pg. 139

viewed as Satan or demons. A writing believed to be from Valentinus, an early gnostic theologian, called *the Gospel of Truth*, states "Speak of the truth with those who seek for it...Do not become a dwelling place for the devil [by speaking blasphemy], for you have already destroyed them." This did not sit well with Irenaeus, another Catholic Church father who lived from the end of the second into the third century CE. He wrote, in response to Valentinus and the like-minded followers of his sect of Christianity, Valentinians, "Let those persons, therefore, who blaspheme the creator...like the Valentinians and all the falsely called gnostics, be recognized as agents of Satan by all who worship God."[192]

A few centuries later, after the idea of who Satan was and what he was not had been bounced around and fought over, the Council of Braga, held in 563 CE, determined the Church's official stance on Satan. Among the positions held, some were convinced that Satan's creation was not done independently of the universe — a position contrary to the dualistic views of other aspects of the faith.[193] It is also thanks to artistic works that we now have concepts of Satan that did not originally exist. For example, John Milton's *Paradise Lost*, a text written in the seventeenth century that offers a creative retelling of the Adam and Eve story, has Satan say, at line 263, "It is better to reign in Hell, than serve in Heaven."

Conclusion

What we can rightly conclude, through the study of scripture, extra-biblical accounts, church fathers, and artistic renderings of

---

[192]Pagels, *the Origin of Satan*, pg. 171, 178
[193]Avalos, *Oxford Guide*, pg. 679

the concept, Hell and Satan, in their current manifestation within our culture, are not biblical by any stretch of the imagination. Hell is the combination of multiple ideas, and ever-shifting beliefs, pooled together to something it was never originally intended to be. We could certainly say the same about Heaven, but as the heavenly realm grew to allow an ease of anxiety for those so needing to be with Yahweh in the next world, so did Hell to alleviate any sense of a possibility for the unfaithful to join the righteous in the next world. Even Satan, who was initially just a vague reference to a person, divine or mortal, started simply to help create a distraction to tempt the follower of Yahweh into deceit against God. He then turned into specific groups that antagonized early Christians, and later into *the* adversary against God, rather than humanity.

In other words, those who followed the Abrahamic faiths, specifically Christianity, made room in Heaven to please their ego, and made Hell an eternity to guarantee their afterlife would not be plagued with those that dissented toward their views.

A concept that was originally meant to, yes, separate the faithful from the oppressors of their people, also still allowed for opportunities for the wicked to repent. People could denounce the views they previously held or, in a worst-case scenario, they would go through a purification period for a maximum of twelve months before joining the righteous. A once-inclusive concept changed, slowly, into an exclusive ideal to ensure there was no salvation available to anyone who did not match their views to the faith of those writing the books now included in the Christian Bible.

Once again, we are faced with circumstances where, we must admit, the original views, even by the later authors of the canonized books of the Bible, are far removed from what modern followers of the faith consider them. This is another clear example of culture shifting and demanding their beliefs shift along with them.

Chapter 3: Resurrection

In the Hebrew Bible

Resurrection is of vital importance to understanding how the views of the afterlife shifted and were shaped in the belief systems of the Jews in antiquity. It is an idea that is, very certainly, something that was conceived after or during the exile in Babylon. It definitely was not a shared ideal, however, as can be seen in early sources like Josephus, who wrote that the Pharisees believed in the immortality of the soul and a resurrection, which was in opposition to the Saducees (*Antiquities* 18.1.3, *War of the Jews* 2.8.14). As a belief, it originated under the exile in Babylon, and persevered under Roman occupation in Palestine. The doctrine of resurrection came about, and persisted, as an association of hope for new life on earth.[194]

The first signs of such a concept are seen in the Book of Job, at 14:13-15: "If mortals die, will they live again? All the days of my service I would wait until my release should come." Although it seems, in context, the author of this section is more interested in having a place to hide in Sheol until God's anger

---

[194]Glasson, *Oxford Guide*, pg. 270-271

passed.[195] Also at 19:25-26, "...and after my skin has been thus destroyed, then in my flesh I shall see God."

This section is not unique to Job; there are several positions that are paralleled in other ancient Near Eastern religions. Part of this comes from the idea of a redeemer calling God to task, which has a parallel in ancient Mesopotamian beliefs that dictated there were mediators, or interceders, between the deity and humanity. It is also reminiscent of a Ugaritic text that states, "And I know that Aleyan Baal is alive."[196]

Job, believed by scholars to have been written during the period of exile,[197] certainly tells the tale of a character who could feel the pain that those in Babylon, the Israelites, could empathize with. Job was someone who had everything he could want and need, until suddenly, and without explanation, all of it is stripped away: his family, land, livestock, wealth, all taken away. But Job maintains his commitment to God, and he is paid back double what he lost.

Ignoring the ethics of a deity that would do this simply to win a bet against a member of his heavenly council, this story is clearly one meant to provide hope for the followers of Yahweh. They have lost a lot, but if they keep their faith and worship him appropriately, they will be rewarded double what they have given up. So it would make sense that, if all else is lost, they still would have the resurrection to look forward to.

[195]Crenshaw, James L., "Job", the Oxford Bible Commentary, Oxford University Press, New York, NY, 2001, pg. 341

[196]Crenshaw, Bible Commentary, pg. 343

[197]Kugler, Robert, and Hartin, Patrick J., An Introduction to the Bible, Wm. B. Eerdmans Publishing, Grand Rapids, MI, 2008, pg. 193

Psalm 49 also offers a different perspective of the concept of the resurrection. The author of this Psalm belittles and antagonizes those that are only concerned with their earthly life and delights, something that was common in the early stages of Judaism. There are remarks about the person going to Sheol, where they are destined to have their home waste away. However, the author notes at verse 15, "But God will ransom my soul from the power of Sheol, for He will receive me." The Hebrew for "take," or "receive" in this instance, comes from the Hebrew word *qabal*, used also in Psalm 73:24, Genesis 5:24, and 2 Kings 2:10. And in these passages, when the word is used, it is done so in a way that implies God taking his loyal servants in to heaven.[198] It is used to refer to Elijah and Elisha's ascent in to heaven.[199] At Psalm 73:24, it reads "You guide me with your counsel, and afterwards you will receive me with honor." Again, this is a recollection and hope for something similar to what happened to Elijah and Elisha. One of the implications, through the context of these passages, was that Sheol was for the wicked. If we remember the discussion about Sheol, it was a place separated from Yahweh; he had no dominion over those who dwelt within the netherworld. So the authors of the Psalms, with at least these two writing during the post-exilic period, felt it was well within their right to dictate that the arrogant, the wicked, go

---

[198]Clifford, Richard J., "Psalms", *the New Oxford Annotated Bible*, Oxford University Press, New York, NY, 2010, pg. 813-814
[199]Rodd, C.S., "Psalms", *the Oxford Bible Commentary*, Oxford University Press, New York, NY, 2001, pg. 381

to Sheol, while the faithful will be received, that is resurrected, into God's kingdom.[200]

There are sections of the Hebrew Bible that mention a person's resurrection, or resuscitation, but these seem to be more on an individual basis, rather than as a promise of an everlasting life in God's kingdom like in the aforementioned passages in Psalms. However, in 1 Kings 17:17-22, we find the story of Elijah reviving a woman's son. It is notable, though, that the child does not come back to life until Elijah cries out, "O Lord my God, let this child's life come into him again." And the child is alive again.

A story from the Ugaritic religion tells followers that the god Baal dies during dry summers and is revived, thanks to his sister, in the fall. This story is meant, more than anything, to showcase that Yahweh is the god of the living, and can even help people escape death.[201] While being part of a continued trend of demonstrating Yahweh's superiority over other "false" deities of multiple Near Eastern faiths, this was very likely not part of the original text and was added in by later editors of 1 Kings. It is also probably written to purposefully be connected to 2 Kings 4:18-37.[202]

There is also 2 Kings 4:32-37, where Elisha prays to God, lies on top of the child until "the flesh of the child became warm" and, as he lay over the child, he sneezed seven times. In this story, the sneezing would signify a return to life and, as

---

[200]"Resurrection" from *the Jewish Encyclopedia*, 1906, retrieved March 19, 2015, http://www.jewishencyclopedia.com/articles/12697-resurrection

[201]Römer, *Oxford Annotated*, pg. 520

[202]Dietrich, Walter, "1 and 2 Kings", *the Oxford Bible Commentary*, Oxford University Press, New York, NY, 2001, pg. 245

Jewish faith dictated, seven was the number of perfection —
similar to how there are seven days in a week and God rested on
the seventh day. [203] Elisha then had the child's mother
summoned, and she took him. This story, likened to the 1 Kings
section we just discussed, is meant more to discuss the power of
God through true, righteous prophets, rather than false ones.
Such a false prophet, named Gehazi, is present in this story,
though probably added at a later date.[204] Again, this is purely on
an individual basis, and not relating to later Jewish ideology
about the afterlife.

Another passage that does relate to the resurrection of the
dead as a collective, and as a part of God's divine plan for the
righteous, is 2 Maccabees 7:9: "And when he was at his last
breath, he said, 'You accursed wretch, you dismiss us from this
present life, but the King of the universe will raise us up to an
everlasting renewal of life, because we have died for his laws.'"
The author of 2 Maccabees wrote during the end of the second
century BCE, and was clearly an educated Jew, as they wrote in
Koine Greek. We know it was written during this time because,
first, it carries the name of Judas Maccabeus, who is the hero of
the piece, who led the Jewish revolt during the mid-second
century BCE. Judging by the time during which we can assume
the piece was written, it is certainly probable that the concept of
resurrection would have been alive and around. We can also tell,
by the use of vocabulary, the narrow range of individuals for
which the resurrection was meant. As a matter of fact, because
of the author's use of first person plural, we can rightfully
assume that they are speaking of an individual resurrection, and

[203]Römer, *Oxford Annotated*, pg. 539
[204]Dietrich, *Bible Commentary*, pg. 250

not yet one of a multitude of people, as later generations would assume.[205]

The author of 2 Maccabees also had a sense of apocalypticism. We can see this when the writer talks about God intervening in human affairs to direct the table of events to a specific point, namely the restoring of the Jewish temple, which had been destroyed during the siege by the Babylonians in the sixth century BCE. And with this, the concept of resurrection becomes a recurring theme, seen also in 12:43-45 and 14:46. However, we are still left with a circumstance that is vague, at best, or only relating to a select few individuals. It is not until we come to the Book of Daniel that we find clear references to a great resurrection.[206]

The Book of Daniel dates to the middle of the second century, BCE. We know this because, among other reasons, the Wisdom of Sirach, a writing dating to 180 BCE, makes reference to every book of the Hebrew Bible except for Daniel. It is written about in the Sibylline Oracles, specifically a particular section dating to the middle of the second century BCE, and also used at Qumran around the same time.[207] Coupled with knowledge of Antiochus IV Epiphanes' campaigns in Egypt

[205]Doran, R., "2 Maccabees", the Oxford Bible Commentary, Oxford University Press, New York, NY, 2001, pg. 734, 742
[206]Schwartz, Daniel R., "2 Maccabees", the New Oxford Annotated Bible, Oxford University Press, New York, NY, 2010, pg. 1613
[207]Hammer, Raymond, the Book of Daniel, Cambridge University Press, Cambridge, UK, 1976, pg. 1-2

between 167-164 BCE, it is reasonable to conclude the author was writing around this time.[208]

Resurrection comes about in Daniel in 12:2: "those who sleep in dust...shall wake, some to everlasting life, some to shame and everlasting contempt." These are ideas that are largely a combination of Judaism with Roman and Greek ideas, thanks to the Hellenistic movement after the death of Alexander the Great in the fourth century BCE. This passage demonstrates a belief that, not only was the soul immortal, but one day it would rejoin the body after death.[209] This idea became so heavily ingrained in the apocalyptic movement of Judaism that, eventually, there was a very blurred line between where Hellenism ended and Judaism began. Paul of Tarsus and his ministry of the coming of God's kingdom and the resurrection of the dead are a perfect example of this.[210]

When Daniel makes a statement about "those who sleep in the dust of the earth," or, more specifically, "the land of dust," this actually meant the bodies of the dead had decayed. They had, in essence, turned to dust. This is, perhaps, in contrast to the Book of Ezekiel, 37:1-14, which makes a reference to "dry bones" and life returning to them. Ezekiel states that, after being preached to, the bones come together, dressed in sinew, and new flesh appears on them. An incredible story, but this one, at least the Ezekiel story, is about Israel overcoming their

---

[208]Collins, John J., *Daniel: With an Introduction to Apocalyptic Literature*, Wm. B. Eerdman's Publishing, Grand Rapids, MI, 1984, pg. 101

[209]White, Sidnie Ann, "Afterlife and Immortality", *the Oxford Guide to the Bible*, Oxford University Press, New York, NY, 1993, pg. 16-17

[210]Roetzel, Calvin J., *the Letters of Paul: Conversation in Context*, Westminster John Knox Press, Louisville, KY, 1998, pg. 46-47

oppressors in Babylon. It is not a literal rising of the dead, as Daniel seems to imply.[211]

What makes Daniel's claim all the more interesting is it does not imply a *physical* rising of the dead. Because the bodies are turning to dust, as the author of Daniel writes, it was more about a transformed, glorified, immortal existence. Similar to 2 Maccabees 7:9, this was not a rising up just out of the ground, this was an implication that the dead would rise up out of Sheol. This was not a physical, but a spiritual body resurrected — one that was not subject to death or decay.[212]

Daniel was writing, and included the concept of resurrection, for a specific reason. Aside from resurrection being an influence from Greek and Roman beliefs that seeped into Judaism, the author, or authors, included the concept of resurrection so that, when God's justice did arrive, both the living *and* the dead could witness it and bask in God's glory. People of the Jewish faith have, seemingly, been met with a lot of persecution, and that continues into the present day. As in Psalm 37, people who follow a faith that suggests the deity they worship is just, will start to wonder just how just that god is. When people of a faith are persecuted, removed from their land, or their homes, are decimated and are forced to worship another deity, to follow another faith or die, followers are bound to start

---

[211]Tabor, James, "Why People are Confused about the earliest Christian View of Resurrection of the Dead?", *TaborBlog*, April 14, 2012, retrieved March 23, 2015, http://jamestabor.com/2012/04/14/why-people-are-confused-about-the-earliest-christian-view-of-resurrection-of-the-dead/

[212]Tabor, James, *Paul and Jesus: How the Apostle Transformed Christianity*, Simon & Schuster, New York, NY, 2012, pg. 57-58

asking questions. Especially when other people, who are viewed as evil, are finding prosperity.

Though Daniel was writing in the second century BCE, he wrote in a way to have the reader believe he was writing from the sixth century BCE, as a well-known Jew who was in exile in Babylon.[213] Daniel's tactic, by implementing such a move, was to attempt to show a level of knowledge of the "future" and a promise of what was to come, by falsely stating he was the Daniel from the exile. Think of Ricky Gervais' character from the movie "The Invention of Lying." In "finding" the ancient text that he actually wrote himself, it helps him to belittle his snarky coworkers and gain the upper hand.[214]

In essence, the author was able to "predict" hardships that were happening to the Jews, even in the second century BCE, and promise good things to happen soon afterwards. Part of this also meant the coming of a resurrection so that the just, both alive and deceased, could revel in the punishment of the unjust. Although it is important to note that Daniel does not say "all" the dead, just "Many of those who have already died," this coincides with the other statement in Daniel 12 that told of some returning to "everlasting contempt." This is perhaps a signifier that those who rose were the faithful Israelites, or perhaps even just those who suffered and died under religious persecution.[215]

---

[213]Reid, Stephen Breck, "the Book of Daniel", *Eerdman's Dictionary of the Bible*, Wm. B. Eerdman's Publishing, Grand Rapids, MI, 2000, pg. 315

[214]*The Invention of Lying*, dir. Ricky Gervais and Matthew Robinson, 2009, Warner Bros.

[215]Nida, *Good News*, pg. 605 & 963

What is perhaps more interesting, not just about Daniel but about the concept of resurrection in general in the Hebrew Bible, is that there is no Hebrew word for "resurrection." It is, as James Tabor has suggested, more akin to "revival," or *chayah*.[216] This would lend further credence to the idea of the dead rising out of Sheol, rather than a bodily resurrection from the ground.[217]

New Testament

Despite there being, really, no word to use in Hebrew that means "resurrection," there most certainly is one in Greek, as used in the New Testament. The word *anastasis*, which would be used to indicate "resurrection", means "a standing up". All in all, it is used 42 times in the New Testament.[218]

And while belief in resurrection appears to be a rather prevalent thought in the early Christian movement, it is also necessary to understand this as part of the Jesus movement in Judaism. This is because Jesus' earliest followers were less concerned with the afterlife and more so with Jesus' return. As can be seen in writings like Mark 9:1, Matthew 16:28, and Luke 9:27, it was expected that Jesus would return, and bring on the end of the age dominated by Roman rule, before the end of his earliest followers' lifetime. "Truly I tell you," Jesus says, "there are some standing here who will not taste death until they see

---

[216]Brown, Driver, Briggs, and Gesenius, "Hebrew Lexicon Entry for Chayah". *the NAS Old Testament*
[217]Tabor, *Paul and Jesus*, pg. 56
[218]Ibid.

that the kingdom of God has come with power." In other words, the end is coming; so be prepared.[219]

Our earliest writings in the New Testament, those of Paul, show a very different view from what someone today might consider a resurrection. Paul's argument for the resurrection can be found, almost in its entirety, in 1 Corinthians 15. Paul's reasoning for arguing for the resurrection, aside from it clearly being something he truly believed in, was because, as he writes at verse 12, some Corinthians believed there was no resurrection to come. Greeks and Romans held tightly to the belief, as sanctioned by popular philosophers inclusive of the oracle at Delphi, that the soul separated from the body at death. So Paul's argument for resurrection is then made by using Plato's *Phaedo* and the argument for the immortality of the soul within.[220]

Paul starts (at verses 1-11) with the resurrection of Jesus and his appearance to Peter, the 12 apostles, to more than 500, to James, all the apostles, and then "Last of all he appeared also to me." With the statement of faith before the list of appearances, this seems to be part of a tradition that was passed down to Paul, as similar statements of faith are made in Romans 4:24-25, 10:9-10, and 1 Thessalonians 5:10. The only change seems to be when Paul states "he was buried" in order to add context for explaining the resurrection.[221] After speaking humbly of himself for a moment, Paul states that he has worked harder than any of

---

[219]Moss, Candida, *the Myth of Persecution: How Early Christians Invented a Story of Martyrdom*, Harper One, New York, NY, 2014, pg. 208, Kindle Edition

[220]Welborne, Laurence L., "the First Letter of Paul to the Corinthians", *the New Oxford Annotated Bible*, Oxford University Press, New York, NY, 2010, pg. 2019-2020

[221]Ibid.

the other apostles. His message turns (at verses 12-34) to the resurrection of the Corinthians and the other faithful who follow Jesus as Messiah. Paul argues "...if the dead are not raised, neither has Christ been raised. And if Christ has not been raised, then your faith is in delusion and you are still lost in your sins."

Rather than a physical body, something one might see in a George A. Romero movie, or on The Walking Dead TV show, Paul's view was that the physical body was left behind — stripped away like dirty clothing. Paul even refers to the spiritual resurrection in 1 Corinthians 15:42-50 (specifically verse 44), "When buried, it is a physical body; when raised, it will be a spiritual body. There is, of course, a physical body, so there has to be a spiritual body." "Spiritual body," however, comes from the Greek *pneumatikos*, which means, literally, "wind body." Paul is so sure in his belief in the spiritual resurrection that he calls those who are unaware of such a circumstance "fools" in the same chapter (verse 36).[222]

Paul also writes, in 1 Thessalonians 4:13-18, that resurrection is guaranteed. We also find this same information shared in Matthew 23:30-43, which, perhaps, suggests a tradition shared between the two authors, or perhaps that Matthew was familiar with Paul's writings.[223] It seems Paul's audience was concerned because people were dying in their community, they wondered if Jesus was not returning, as Paul preached, to save

---

[222]Tabor, "Christian View of Resurrection", *Tabor Blog*, retrieved March 23, 2015, http://jamestabor.com/2012/04/14/why-people-are-confused-about-the-earliest-christian-view-of-resurrection-of-the-dead/

[223]Horrell, David G., "the First Letter of Paul to the Thessalonians", *the New Oxford Annotated Bible*, Oxford University Press, New York, NY, 2010, pg. 2078

humanity and return God's kingdom to earth. Paul tells them, "...the dead in Christ will rise first. Then we who are alive, who are left, will be caught up in the clouds together with them to meet the Lord in the air; and so we will be with the Lord forever."

Paul's words were meant as reassurance; the Thessalonians were concerned that their loved ones who had passed away would not be able to witness the glory of Jesus' return. So what better way to offer peace of mind than informing congregants that the dead will bask in his glory first.[224] It is clear, through this letter as well as others Paul had written, that hope, or *elpis* in Greek, was one of the central tenets of the faith that Paul preached. We see this at 1 Thessalonians 1:3, where Paul tells the Thessalonians that "hope" is not only a vital part of being a follower of Christ, but it also separated those in the Jesus movement from other faiths. While it is clearly a false idea, to assume that no one of any other faith had hope, it is a large part of Paul's game plan to help assure them that the resurrection is coming, and all will be included.[225]

Unfortunately for the Thessalonians, Paul more or less offers the same time frame for the end as Jesus. In 1 Thessalonians 5, Paul says it is unnecessary to let them know when the day will come, "For you yourselves know very well that the Day of the Lord will come as a thief comes at night...'Everything is quiet and safe,' then suddenly destruction will hit them! It will come as suddenly as the pains that come upon a woman in labor, and people will not escape." In Mark

[224]Nida, *Good News*, pg. 1594
[225]Esler, Philip F., "1 Thessalonians", *the Oxford Bible Commentary*, Oxford University Press, New York, NY, 2001, pg. 1209

13:30-32, Jesus says, "Truly I tell you, this generation will not pass away until all these things [the coming of God's kingdom] have taken place...But about that day or hour no one knows, neither the angels in heaven, nor the Son, but only the Father." Even before the New Testament books were being constructed, the author of Isaiah wrote that "on that day a great trumpet will be blown, and those who were lost in the land of Assyria and those who were driven out of the land of Egypt will come and worship the LORD on the holy mountain at Jerusalem." Zephaniah, giving a more bleak depiction of "that day," wrote that "the sound of the day of the LORD is bitter, the warrior cries aloud there. That day will be a day of wrath, a day of distress and anguish...in the fire of his passion the whole earth shall be consumed..." It seems likely, given how well versed Paul was in the Septuagint, that he would have imparted this information to the churches he established, especially since they were Gentiles, or non-Jews. This would have been to help them feel their decision to join the faith was a good one, and that those who did not join the faith were doomed.[226] So both Paul and the author of Mark are consistent in believing that the end, which Paul suggests will bring about the *anastasis*, will happen soon, but they do not know when.

About twenty years later, the Gospel of Mark, the earliest gospel account of the four that were canonized, had a Jesus that was very much an apocalyptic preacher. With this gospel we find passages like, "Truly I tell you, there are some here who will not die until they have seen the Kingdom of God come with power." This is at Mark 9:1. Mark 13 is also referred to as the "mini-apocalypse." This is because, throughout this chapter,

---

[226]Esler, *Bible Commentary*, pg. 1210

Jesus makes remarks about the troubles the followers of Jesus will see, the destruction of the Jerusalem Temple, false prophets, and, you guessed it, the coming end of the rule of man, which will bring in God's kingdom on earth.[227]

In Mark 5:41-43, we are met with the story of a man named Jairus who has an ill daughter. When Jesus goes to heal her, he finds that she has died during his travels. This story is retold in Luke, and in Matthew Jairus' daughter is already dead when Jesus is asked to come see her. When Jesus does find her, and sees people grieving, he says, "'Why all this confusion? Why are you crying? The child is not dead-she is only sleeping!'...He took her by the hand and said to her, '*Talitha koum*,' which [in Aramaic] means, 'Little girl, I tell you to get up!'" It is interesting, first, that Jesus tells the witnesses that are grieving that Jairus' daughter is sleeping. I say this because to "sleep," in some biblical passages, also means to die. Most importantly, for our purposes, in Daniel 12:2, "Many of those who sleep in the dust of the earth shall awake..." I say that this is more important because Jesus very clearly has an apocalyptic mind frame that parallels Daniel, inclusive of death, resurrection, and judgment.

It is also crucial to know that the age of Jairus' daughter, 12 (5:42), is an important number. We note this because it is relevant to the story just before, regarding a woman who was hemorrhaging for 12 years (5:25). Twelve is a relevant number as it was the number of sons descended from Jacob, who was later named *Israel*, and each represented a different tribe of Israel (Genesis 35). Jesus also had 12 disciples, 12 unleavened cakes were to be laid out each week for God on the Sabbath (Leviticus

---

[227]Davidson, John, *the Gospel of Jesus: In Search of His Original Teachings*, Clear Press, Ltd., Bristol, UK, 2005, pg. 525-526

24), and, when we get to Revelation, there are 12,000 from each tribe that will receive salvation (chapter seven), another group of 144,000 (12 x 12,000) that will be taken to serve Jesus (14:1-5), and the bride of Christ will have a crown with 12 stars on it in chapter 12. The number, at least in Mark, is pertinent because it is meant to show Jesus' ability to renew Israel.[228]

More than anything else, analyzing this story, along with the one about the hemorrhaging woman a few verses before, we see a theme of faith saving people. Faith is responsible for stopping the woman's bleeding, as Jesus states at 5:34, and Jesus tells Jairus when he doubts, "Don't be afraid, only believe." Lo and behold, because of their faith, Jesus is able to provide a miracle. So aside from being stories that show a close relationship to the concept of the 12 tribes of Israel, these passages show that the miracle is performed, and, hence, the people can be saved because of faith.[229] Similar ideas are seen in Mark 16:15-16: "Go into all the world and proclaim the gospel to the whole creation. Whoever believes and is baptized will be saved, but whoever does not believe will be condemned." John 5:24 shares this idea, "Truly, I say to you, whoever hears my word and believes him who sent me has eternal life."

The raising of Jairus' daughter might also be considered a moment of what is called "realized eschatology," or a glimmer of the end of the age. We certainly see a lot more of this in the Gospel of John, as Jesus performs a number of miracles indicating that not only is the end imminent, it has already started to happen, according to the authors. John 3:18 even

---

[228]Horsley, *Oxford Annotated*, pg. 1801
[229]Keene, Michael, *Saint Mark's Gospel and the Christian Faith*, Nelson Thornes, Cheltenham, UK, 2002. pg. 72

states that one who does not believe "stands condemned already." John 5:24, aside from what has been said already, also says "[whoever believes] will not be judged but has crossed over from death to life." And we see an example in John's gospel, at chapter 11 with the resurrection of Lazarus. A rising of the dead also occurs in Matthew 27:53, with the saints emerging from their tombs in Jerusalem after Jesus dies on the cross. This implies, through Matthew's logic, that the "day of the Lord,", as mentioned in Paul's writings and in Isaiah and Zephaniah, has happened; the first fruits of God's kingdom, which Paul also writes about (1 Corinthians 15:20), have been raised and collected. [230] So, it would make sense that, with a book so focused on the coming end of Roman rule and beginning of God's rule on earth, there would be a moment of realized eschatology to insinuate that God's kingdom was coming soon.[231]

In the Gospel of Luke 7:11-17, Jesus encounters a widow's son at Nain who had died and was being carried out. "Then he came forward and touched the bier, and the bearers stood still. And he said, 'Young man, I say to you, rise!' The dead man sat up and began to speak, and Jesus gave him to his mother." This story would be incredible, but we know it is a repetition of the Elijah story in 1 Kings 17:17-24. In fact, the resemblance to the Elijah story is so well noted that even the audience in the story reacts strongly. "Fear seized all of them; and they glorified God, saying 'A great prophet has risen among us!'" The story also has a parallel in Acts, written by the same author as Luke, at 9:36-42

[230]Allison, Dale C., Jr., "Matthew", the Oxford Bible Commentary, Oxford University Press, New York, NY, 2001, pg. 884
[231]Kysar, Robert, John, the Maverick Gospel, Presbyterian Publishing Corp, Louisville, KY, pg. 119-120

when the apostle Peter raises Tabitha.[232] Being that these stories are only found in Luke and Acts, and with the close parallels to suggest the stories were directly linked to the Elijah story in 1 Kings, it is safe to assume the author used it more as a theological implication that Jesus was connected to the prophet Elijah.

In the Gospel of John, written at the end of the first century CE, we find the well-known, but unique to John, story of the resurrection of Lazarus. Prior to the story of Lazarus' resurrection, John's gospel is dripping with realized eschatology; this includes John 4:21-24, "But the hour is coming, and is now here..." Even in the well-known passage of John 3:16 and the surrounding verses, there are implications of a realized promise that is antithetical to dying, "...so that everyone who believes in him may not perish but may have eternal life...Those who believe in him are not condemned; but those who do not believe are condemned already...And this is the judgment..." Even at 5:24, "anyone who hears my words and believes him who sent me has eternal life, and does not come under judgment, but has passed from death to life." This was not only to imply a message of a present eschatological time for the characters in John's narrative, but also to inform the reader of John's gospel, 60 years or so removed from the time of Jesus' actual ministry, that they are living in the actual end of the age.[233]

John has, very thoroughly, set the stage for the reader to understand that the end is not coming, but already here. And

---

[232]Franklin, Eric, "Luke", *the Oxford Bible Commentary*, Oxford University Press, New York, NY, 2001, pg. 935
[233]Michaels, J. Ramsey, *the New International Commentary on the New Testament: the Gospel of John*, Wm. B. Eerdman's Publishing, Grand Rapids, MI, 2010, pg. 252-253

with that, it sets up an easy opening to get the Lazarus story into the gospel narrative. Even prior to this, at John 5:25, Jesus lets his audience know that "the hour is coming, and is now here, when the dead will hear the voice of the Son of God, and those who hear will live." So, when Jesus gets to the tomb where Lazarus is laid, after consoling his sisters Mary and Martha, he goes to the tomb and calls out, "Lazarus, come out!" And Lazarus rises and comes out of the tomb.

Interestingly, this is supposed to be the pinnacle of Jesus' ministry, at least according to the gospel author. We see this at the end of chapter 11 (verses 45-57), when some who had witnessed the resurrection of Lazarus go to the Pharisees, which starts the wheels turning to have Jesus crucified. This is in light of John 2:4, when Jesus' mother (unnamed in the Gospel of John) informs him that they had run out of wine at the wedding in Cana. Jesus' response is, "My time has not yet come." He was reluctant to perform any miracles, even as minute as turning water to wine, as he did not want to show any signs until it was time for his death.[234] We cannot look at these events and assume they are historically accurate as, among other reasons, these are unique to the Gospel of John and this particular account is among the latest contributed to the Christian canon. With that in mind, it is clear that this story was set up as part of the developing faith of some of the earliest followers of Jesus rather than a historical retelling of events during his ministry.[235]

What is more telling, and interesting to note, is the time that elapses between Jesus' notification of Lazarus' illness, Lazarus'

---

[234]Nida, *Good News*, pg. 1424
[235]Vermes, Geza, *Christian Beginnings: From Nazareth to Nicaea*, Yale University Press, New Haven, CT, 2013, pg. 35

death, and when Jesus arrives to bring him back from the dead. At the end of chapter 10, we learn that Jesus had returned to the Jordan River "where John had been baptizing..." A problem arises trying to understand where Bethany is located. Is Bethany located in modern day al-Eizariya on the West Bank[236] or on the east side of the Jordan River, the very location where John the Baptist was located? According to John 1:28; "All this happened in Bethany on the east side of the Jordan River, where John was baptizing." It is interesting, but it is also noted in most commentaries that this is not the same location, as the real name of the city John was baptizing in was "Bethabara" or "Betharaba."[237] However, if we look at the traditional spot for the city of Bethany and plan a route out to the Jordan River, it would take roughly 26 hours straight to reach it, making it feasible to believe that this trip could have been made in the two days it is alleged that Jesus and his followers took to make it there. This is also after two days of waiting: "Jesus loved Martha and her sister and Lazarus. Yet when he received the news that Lazarus was sick, he stayed where he was for two more days. Then he said to the disciples, 'Let us go back to Judea.'" They make the two-day trip, despite the apostles not understanding that Jesus had said Lazarus was dead. Historically, this would have made little sense.

First, Jesus says Lazarus "has fallen asleep," from the Greek *koimao*, which is another way of saying that he has died. This language is used numerous times in the Bible, including in 1 Corinthians 15:18, 1 Thessalonians 4:14, Matthew 9:24, Acts 7:60, and so on. Even in Hebrew, *radam*, the word literally

[236]Shahin, Mariam, *Palestine: A Guide*, Interlink Books, Northampton, MA, 2005, pg. 332
[237]Nida, *Good News*, pg. 1423

translates into "to fall asleep," but meant death. Jesus and the disciples would have spoken Aramaic, a language that derived from Hebrew, and the term would have been understood to refer to death.[238]

So they proceed back to find Lazarus dead, and having been dead for four days. This means he likely was dead at the time Jesus had received the message, which would make Martha's argument, "If you had been here, Lord, my brother would not have died," rather insignificant. So Jesus goes and wakes him up, or raises him from the dead. But why is four days significant? It is because, if we read the Talmud, Genesis Kabbah 100:7, it is stated that the soul of the deceased stayed with or near the body for three days. During this time, *shomrim*, Hebrew for "guards", watched over the body and read psalms aloud in order to provide comfort to both the body and the soul. After three days, the soul descended into Sheol. So, by Jesus waiting an extra few days, and by not reaching the tomb until Lazarus' soul would have been believed to have descended into Sheol where God could not reach him, Jesus did a tremendous thing that not even God could have done.[239]

In Revelation, 20:4-13, we read about more dead rising.

"*They came to life and ruled as kings with Christ...The rest of the dead did not come to life until the thousand years were over. This is the first raising of the dead. Happy and greatly blessed are those who are included in this first raising of the dead. The second death has no power over them...Then the sea gave up the dead they held. And all were judged according to what they had done.*"

---

[238]Nida, *Good News*, pg. 1439
[239]Raphael, *Jewish Views*, pg. 140

This passage obviously seems out of sorts since judgment happens a verse *before* the resurrection from the sea. The author had meant it as a means to emphasize judgment on a universal level — applying to both the living and the dead, and then the dead who had no sufficient or proper burial.[240]

A problem we run into with this passage, and others in the New Testament, is the question of what the resurrected body is supposed to consist of. As we see in the section of Revelation, those who are lost at sea, or receive improper burials, are physically resurrected. Even in Luke 24:39, Jesus, having just risen from the dead, says, "Look at my hands and my feet, and see that it is I myself. Feel me, and you will know, *for a ghost doesn't have flesh and bones, as you can see I have.*" Luke, traditionally believed to have been a companion of the apostle Paul, seems to have a strange view of the body post-resurrection. Luke includes this passage to strongly emphasize the real physicality of Jesus' resurrection, something that Paul, if we read his letters, was completely against.[241]

Paul writes, at 1 Corinthians 15:44, "When buried, it is a physical body; when raised, it will be a spiritual body." Paul had even written in Galatians 1:15-16 that Jesus' resurrection was a "divine revelation," rather than a physical appearance.[242] Despite what Acts of the Apostles states, the story of Paul's conversion on the road to Damascus is not reciprocated anywhere in Paul's writings.

---

[240]Mounce, Robert H., *the New International Commentary on the New Testament: the Book of Revelation*, Wm. B. Eerdman's Press, Grand Rapids, MI, 1998, Kindle Edition, Loc 6875 of 12986
[241]Franklin, Eric, "Luke", *the Oxford Bible Commentary*, Oxford University Press, New York, NY, 2001, pg. 958
[242]Nida, *Good News*, pg. 1560

Also included in Paul's writings is 2 Corinthians 5:16-17, where the author says, "From now on, therefore, we regard no one according to the flesh, even though we once regarded Christ according to the flesh, *we regard him such no longer*." [Emphasis my own] So here, again, we see Paul talking about Jesus as no longer a person of the flesh. This may be why, in all of Paul's writings, we see nothing about the earthly life of Jesus — his message, ministry, miracles, nothing of his life up until his crucifixion. We hear he was born "of a woman," was crucified, and was raised from the dead. That is all we know of Jesus' life from Paul's writings.[243]

What is more interesting is that Paul closes his discussion of the final resurrection of the dead into God's kingdom with "flesh and blood will not inherit the kingdom of God" at 15:50. He says, in so many words, that a physical resurrection is *impossible*.[244] The difference is in knowing that humanity wears the symbol of Adam, the *psyche* or body animated by a soul, but when people pass away they shall bear the symbol of Jesus, the *pneuma* that originated in heaven and is immortal.[245] Aside from our bearing the mark of Adam, this view of resurrection is also perpetuated because the physical human body was susceptible to decay and death, as opposed to the spiritual *pneuma,* which would flourish in the perfection of God's kingdom.[246]

Paul's own view on resurrection, and whether one was resurrected as a spirit or in a physical body, appears to emulate

---

[243]Tabor, *Paul and Jesus*, pg. 132

[244]Welborne, *New Oxford*, pg. 2021

[245]Barclay, *Oxford Annotated*, pg. 1132

[246]Fee, Gordon D., *the New International Commentary on the New Testament: the First Epistle to the Corinthians*, Wm. B. Eerdman's Publishing, Grand Rapids, MI, 1987, pg. 799

the idea put forward by Plato. Namely, Plato felt, as he detailed in his book *Phaedo*, that the body was an "earthly prison." And, given the philosophy Plato held on life coming from death, he felt that a resurrection of the spirit, rather than the spiritual body, was more likely.[247] So, if the soul was freed from its earthly prison, why would it have any desire to return?

What is clearly observed, by reading and understanding the various resurrection stories in the Bible, is that each one is told with a specific reason in mind. Whether it is for the purpose of offering a promise of a reborn, stronger Israel that would overthrow their unjust captors in the exile in Babylon, or if it meant a return of God's kingdom on earth to stop the tyrannical Roman rule in the Jews' sacred land of Israel, even if it was to show that what a small sect of Jews felt was God's son, the Messiah, was on earth to reign in the end of an era. Resurrection was done, or written about, with an agenda in mind — with a purpose. And it meant a coming judgment.[248]

After the Bible

I would like to, first, point out a slight distinction between resurrection and what is known as "apotheosis." Apotheosis is when a person, after their death, is taken into heaven and divinized. We see examples of this in the writings of Suetonius — specifically *the Twelve Caesars* (Penguin Books, 1957). At 1.88, Suetonius writes, "a comet appeared about an hour before sunset...This was held to be Caesar's soul, elevated to heaven;

---

[247] Connolly, Tim, "Plato: Phaedo" *The Internet Encyclopedia of Philosophy,* http://www.iep.utm.edu/phaedo/#SH3b, East Stroudsburg University, Stroudsburg, PA
[248] Moss, *Myth of Persecution*, pg. 208

hence the star, now placed above the forehead of his divine image." Suetonius also writes of similar instances of apotheosis with Emperors Vespasian at verse 23, and Claudius at verse 46.

In terms of actual resurrection, we do have a few accounts of such an event after the biblical era. One example is Rabbi Judah I, also known as Judah the Prince. He was one of the main editors and redactors of the Mishnah and an important leader of the Jewish community during Rome's occupation of Judea. It was reported that, after his death in 220 CE, he would return home "at twilight every Sabbath Eve."[249]

In the seventeenth century, a Jewish teacher who claimed he was the Messiah, Sabbatai Zevi, is also alleged to have returned from the dead. His resurrection was marked by an empty tomb, though guarded by a dragon, and some of his followers alleged Zevi never died. He only appeared to do so.[250] A similar belief was held by a gnostic sect of early Christianity called "Docetism," from the Greek *dokein* meaning "to appear."

Resurrection was also something Maimonides, a Jewish philosopher, physician, and astronomer, adapted into his *Thirteen Principles of Faith*, which included, among others, God's awareness of human action, the coming of the Jewish Messiah, and that the Torah, as he had it in his day, was the one God had dictated to Moses. In the Jewish faith, as it just so happens,

---

[249]Slotki, Israel W., editor, *the Babylonian Talmud (Seder Nashim, Kethuboth), Vol. III*, translated by S. Daiches, Rebecca Bennett Publications, Inc., 1959, XIII.103A
[250]Scholem, Gershom, *Sabbatai Sevi: the Mystical Messiah*, Princeton University Press, Princeton, NJ, 1973, pg. 917-929

denial of the resurrection of the dead was viewed as heretical until the modern Reform period.[251]

In Christianity, the resurrection stayed around, and is still kicking today. Even the Nicene Creed, the profession of faith established at the Council of Nicaea in 325 CE, states, "We look for the resurrection of the dead, and the life of the world to come." It was made clear, thanks to early Church fathers like Justin Martyr, that it was not just a spiritual resurrection, like Paul taught in his letters. Martyr writes, in order to protest those who say there will be no physical resurrection, that "these persons seek to rob the flesh of the promise." He also uses Mark 12:25 as proof of a bodily resurrection, claiming that "[the dead] neither marry nor are given in marriage, but are like angels in heaven."[252]

In spite of all of this, some theologians had adverse reactions to the idea of the resurrection. This included people like Augustine of Hippo, who, in his *Sermon on Psalm 88*, wrote, "No doctrine of the Christian faith is so vehemently and so obstinately opposed as the doctrine of the resurrection of the flesh."[253]

---

[251]Wigoder, Geoffrey, "Resurrection", *the New Standard Jewish Encyclopedia, 7th Edition,* Facts on File, Inc., New York, NY, 1992, pg. 797
[252]Martyr, Justin, *Fragments of the Lost Work of Justin on the Resurrection*, translated by the Rev. M. Dods, MA, edited by Rev. Alexander Roberts and James Donaldson, T&T Clark, Edinburgh, Scotland, 1886, retrieved April 22, 2015, http://www.mb-soft.com/believe/txv/martyr7.htm
[253]Maas, Anthony, "General Resurrection", *the Catholic Encyclopedia*, the Robert Appleton Co., New York, NY, 1911, retrieved April 22, 2015, http://www.newadvent.org/cathen/12792a.htm

When Lutheran, or Protestant, Christianity emerged, the common view was that the soul would be reunited with the body at the resurrection at the end of days.[254] And so, as we can see, we are teetering back-and-forth with the view of either a physical or spiritual resurrection, but maintaining that, still, one happens.

Conclusion

As recently as just a week ago at the time of writing, a couple in Texas were on the run after purposefully starving a child, a toddler, that they thought was possessed by a demon. When the attempted resurrection failed, they wrapped the child in a blanket and tried to bring him to Mexico.[255] This was not just something that faced us in the ancient world. For a time, in fact, there was even a law requiring that, when the dead were buried, they must be so with their heads facing west and their feet to the east so that, when the resurrection happened, they would be ready to meet Jesus.[256]

This is, however, such a far cry from the original concept of resurrection. First, to consider it was meant as a spiritual rising, makes such laws as the one with the specific directions in order to rise and meet Jesus now sounds outrageous. It also completely contradicts the Book of Daniel and the writings of

---

[254]Graebner, Augustus Lawrence, *Outlines of Doctrinal Theology*, Concordia Publishing, St. Louis, MO, 1911, pg. 233

[255]Johnson, M. Alex, "Texas Woman Arrested In Alleged Attempt to Resurrect Dead Toddler", *NBC News*, April 13, 2015, retrieved April 22, 2015, http://www.nbcnews.com/news/us-news/texas-woman-arrested-alleged-attempt-resurrect-dead-toddler-n340976

[256]Olcott, William Tyler, *Sun Lore of All Ages*, G. P. Putnam's Sons, New York, NY, 1914, pg. 143

Paul. It is passages, like the one in Luke, that completely deviate from the original concept that start to give creative license to those who wish to interpret it differently.

While not necessarily a change that was a derivative of shifts in culture, as the modifications to heaven and Hell were, the back and forth between physical and spiritual resurrection shows the struggle in philosophical differences. It presents us with what is known as "the Cartesian argument" for the soul. And that will provide an excellent merger into our next topic: the soul.

Chapter 4: Soul

In the Hebrew Bible

In the Hebrew Bible, we are met with a couple of instances of discussion about the soul. Near the very beginning of the Bible, in Genesis 2:7, the King James Version reads, "And the LORD God formed man of the dust of the ground, and breathed into his nostrils the breath of life; and man became a living soul." The problem, here, is that "soul" is mistranslated and should read, instead, "living being." It comes from the Hebrew word *nefesh*, which translates, literally, to "breathing creature." This word is used numerous times in Genesis, often coupled with *hayyah*, like at 1:24 and 7:15, to refer to various animals that are with the same "breath of life." And though it is used, more often than not, in reference to living things, we also see the word *nefesh* used in reference to the dead at Numbers 9:7: "Although we are unclean from touching a dead corpse [*nefesh*]..."[257] It is also seen at Numbers 6:6, which states that "[a]ll the days that they separate themselves from the LORD they shall not go near a dead corpse." In this instance, as is the case with Leviticus 21:11, the word *nefesh* is paired with *met*.[258]

Nefesh, along with other words that were synonymous with it (*ruah* and *neshamah*), was used to indicate life through the animation of the body; though the root of the word, as

[257]Tabor, *Paul and Jesus*, pg. 52-53
[258]Raphael, *Jewish Views*, pg. 56

suggested before, was "wind" or "breath." Despite there being a suggestion of an animated spirit, the view was, upon death, the person led a shadow-like life in Sheol.[259] The dead would retain their form, and even their consciousness and memory of what had happened in their lives. They were even, to an extent, cognizant of what was happening, still, in the lives of their living families.[260]

Although the word *nefesh* is used to address predominantly animal life, which might make us pause to consider how biblical authors perhaps viewed humanity the same way biologists do, we can see a distinction between *nefesh* and *ruah* in the Book of Job. At Job 12:7-10, it reads, "In his hands is the life [*nefesh*] of every living thing and the spirit [*ruah*] of every human being." This passage, while seemingly implying that only mankind has a spirit, actually is meant to demonstrate that all animals are imbued with the spirit, or the breath of God.[261] It is just the spirit of every human that is in God's hands. Perhaps this is meant as a reference back to Genesis 1:26, where it says, "Let us make humankind in our image...and let them have dominion over the fish of the sea, and over the birds of the air, and over the cattle, and over all the wild animals of the earth."

What we must accept is that the Israelites did not have a dualistic approach to the body-soul dynamic, like Greek philosophers did. In other words, the combination of a fleshy body and spirit, or soul, did not determine the sum of the parts

---

[259]Wigoder, Geoffrey, "Soul", *the New Standard Jewish Encyclopedia*, Facts on File, Inc., New York, NY, 1992, pg. 880
[260]McDannell and Lang, *Heaven: A History*, pg. 6
[261]Wright, Archie T., "the Spirit in Early Jewish Interpretation: Examining John R. Levinson's Filled With the Spirit", *Pneuma Journal of the Society for Pentecostal Studies, Vol. 33*, Issue 1, pg. 37

of the nature of life.[262] It can only be found, in the Jewish faith, through Jewish mysticism, like Kabbala, and the gnostic and theosophical sects of Judaism. We see these later concepts in 1 Enoch, where the author talks about angels being cast out of heaven for marrying the daughters of earth — a story calling on the tradition from Genesis 6 with Noah and the flood. Also, in the Qumran texts from the Dead Sea Scrolls, it is said that "he created man to have dominion over the world and made for him two spirits; so that he may walk by them until the time of his visitation..."[263]

The idea of a shadowed, gloomy figure in the netherworld, a rather depressing one, was the standard belief leading up to the Babylonian exile. Before that, from the tenth to the eighth century BCE, there was no philosophy of the soul, let alone a judgment like is depicted in Revelation. A person, after using up their *nefesh*, or the "wind" or "breath" that animated their body, continued their lives in Sheol.[264] This changed dramatically after the Jewish people went through the exile. After that time, it was no longer acceptable to think that, when they passed on to the next world, Jews would be met with a dark and gloomy afterlife. What is more, it was absurd to think they would share in that realm with the very people who put them in captivity.

As we discussed with Paul in the section regarding Hell, the Jews appeared to have a more annihilationist perspective on the

---

[262]Hare, Douglas R.A., "Flesh and Spirit", *the Oxford Guide to the Bible*, Oxford University Press, New York, NY, 1993, pg. 231

[263]Stefon, Matt, "dualism", *the Encyclopaedia Brittanica Online*, 2015, retrieved April 23, 2015, http://www.britannica.com/EBchecked/topic/172631/dualism/38203/Anthropological-functions

[264]Raphael, *Jewish Views*, pg. 57

soul, prior to Hellenization. While we may see something resembling the concept of a life beyond death in the Book of Job, Job was written relatively late in the Jewish biblical period, whereas Ezekiel and Jeremiah (which predate Job) make absolutely no reference to a soul, let alone a sense of an immortal spirit beyond death.[265] Ecclesiastes (3:19-20) supports this view as well, "All go to one place; all are from the dust, and all return to dust again." The author even questions, in the next verse, whether man's soul goes into the heavens and animals' go into the earth. At 12:7 of Ecclesiastes, the author writes that, upon death, the body returns to dust and the *nefesh* in them returns to God.[266] It is the annihilationist belief — that the righteous live and prosper, and the wicked die and cease to be. Even if belief in a soul existed, it certainly did not take a prominent place in the belief system until after biblical times.

Enter Hellenistic Judaism, the faith inspired by the philosophers and authors of the Greeks. Philo of Alexandria, as an example, played a heavy hand in helping to advance and develop the concept of the soul in Jewish thought. Philo, taking his cues from Greek intellects in the same vein as Plato and Cicero, introduced the idea of an immortal, immaterial, and, interestingly, an a-sexual soul. Though this version of the soul did become a strong part of the belief system during this time, Philo also helped introduce the view into Judaism that Moses, and only Moses, entered the higher realm with God.[267] This is an interesting thought, given what is now believed about the soul and those that dwell in the heavenly realm.

---

[265]Raphael, *Jewish Views*, pg. 63-64
[266]Tabor, *Paul and Jesus*, pg. 53
[267]McDannell and Lang, *Heaven: A History*, pg. 15-18

Philo's views certainly helped influence the writer of the Book of Wisdom. Like in chapter three, where it says, "The souls of the righteous are in the hands of God...their passing away was thought an affliction and their going forth from us utter destruction. But they are in peace."

After the Yahweh Alone movement, which we discussed earlier, even when there was a belief in spirits, the idea of communicating with the dead was cut off in order to ensure people were worshipping Yahweh and no one else. Because they were venerating their ancestors, it was viewed as a form of idol worship to communicate with the dead, potentially leading to the law in Leviticus 20:27, which promoted stoning for the crime of communicating with the dead. Strangely enough, it was required that the living must listen to Moses and the prophets.[268] Perhaps Moses is understandable, given what is believed about Moses going directly to the heavenly realm with God. Regardless, were the prophets not viewed as humans who had died?

Not only did the soul become a prominent idea, but, in the last centuries before the Common Era, the soul was also viewed as an entity, or substance, independent from the body. Another view said that said the soul, being immortal, has always existed and joins with the body upon conception. The Talmud, a central text to Rabbinic Judaism, also accepts the immortality of the soul and the idea that it joins the body upon conception. There is even a theory that, when a person sins, it is not the body, but the soul that sins.[269] This is an idea that is the complete opposite of what later theologians and moralists would have followers of

[268]McDannell and Lang, *Heaven: A History*, pg. 28
[269]Wigoder, "Soul", pg. 880

the faith believe. The latter is something that we see as we turn to the New Testament and Paul of Tarsus' view on the body and soul dynamic.

New Testament

Prior to Christianity, or what would become Christianity, the Jews had felt that soul and body were synonymous with one another; yes, there was a physical body, and certainly there was a soul, but they were not distinct from one another. When Hellenism reached Israel, and seeped its way into the beliefs and literature of the Jews, it took on the philosophies of Plato and his followers — namely that the body was, to some extent, just an appendage, and a temporary one at that.[270]

In *Phaedo*, Plato is recounting Socrates' final moments before his death. Plato, while having written pieces like *Gorgias* that detail the dead coming to a meadow to be judged according to their deeds (sounds familiar), has Socrates say:

"*...is not part of us body and the rest of us soul? ...the soul is the very like-ness of the divine, and immortal and intelligible and uniform, and indissoluble, and unchangeable; and the body is in the very likeness of the human and unintelligible, and multiform, and dissoluble, and changeable ...the soul when attacked by death cannot perish...the soul will not admit of death, or even be dead, any more than three or the odd number will admit of the even.*"

With these views in mind, Christianity tried their best to attempt to merge the two philosophies. Sadly, it was a very poor mixing that they did.[271]

---

[270]Russell, *A History of Heaven*, pg. 19
[271]Ibid.

As we discussed with the concept of the resurrection, there were two views of the body in apocalyptic thought. There was the future resurrected body, as we saw in the resurrection story in Luke 24:41-53, and then there was the transformation into a spiritual body, as is seen in Paul's first letter to the Corinthians. Paul, interestingly enough, did feel that there were spiritual bodies, but he claimed that they would remain in a peaceful slumber until the great resurrection. As we see in 1 Thessalonians 4:13-5:10, Paul describes the slumber of death as a peaceful sleep. It is absolutely known that the term "to fall asleep" also means "to die," and in this case Paul uses the metaphor in a semi-literal way; this is to demonstrate that, unlike those who did not believe, or belittled those who did, their punishment will be in Gehenna, or in the fires, while the righteous wait peacefully until the parousia. [272] According to Paul, even if a soul is real, it would wait peacefully with the body that with which it was buried and not haunt old houses or speak to us through mediums.

In the gospel accounts, we need to make some distinctions. First, demons, like the ones Jesus exorcises out of people, are not what we are looking for. And, given our discussion on Hell and Satan, I believe we already have the demons covered. That aside, it is difficult to speak of spirits in these writings because, in instances where there has been a death, Jesus resurrects the person. In Luke we have Jairus' daughter resurrected. In Matthew we see that the saints after Jesus' death were resurrected — they also entered the city and "appeared to many". In John we have Lazarus, who was also resurrected. In all four, Jesus himself is resurrected, and we know from Luke

[272]Reicke, "Hell", *Oxford Guide*, pg. 278

that it is in a physical body. Only once do we see any persons that one might assume would be spirits, Elijah and Moses in Matthew 17:1-13 (and the parallel accounts; Mark 9:2-13 and Luke 9:28-36), during the transfiguration. Only one problem arises: according to biblical tradition, though Moses was believed to be dead (Deuteronomy 34), Elijah was carried up to heaven in a chariot of fire (2 Kings 2:8)! We never get a detailed account as to whether they were *pneuma*, or spiritual bodies, or physical bodies.

Instead of looking at this in a literal sense, we need to see what the authors were trying to say. In this instance, Jesus is shown to play an important role within the faith to the ever-so-oblivious disciples. Jesus is transformed at the top of a mountain, very much like God's revelation to Moses on Sinai/Horeb. It is done in front of Jesus' three closest apostles, Peter, James, and John, and they see these three together — two of them representing the law and the prophets of the Hebrew Bible. It is also a call back to a passage in Malachi 4:5 where it says Elijah will come before the day of the Lord. [273] After numerous instances of creating parallels between Jesus and Moses, it is hard to take a lot of the Gospel of Matthew seriously or literally.

There are, indeed, a few places we may consider the authors of the gospels, and Acts, to be speaking of a supernatural spirit. If we look at Acts 7:59, we find the stoning of the first Christian martyr, Stephen. Before he dies, he says, "Lord Jesus, receive my spirit." This certainly fits the expectation of a separate, ethereal entity. But, this is actually a call back to Jesus' statement on the cross right before he dies at Luke 23:46, "Father, into your

---

[273] Cousland, "Matthew", *Oxford Annotated*, pg. 1771

hands I commend my spirit!" Even more interesting is this statement, whether you wish to consider this an original part of Luke or something taken from Mark 15:40-41, is actually a reference to Psalms 31:5. In this passage, the psalmist writes, "Into your hand I commit my spirit." The Hebrew word used for "spirit" here is *ruhi*, which derives from *ruah*. In context of the psalm, especially since it is a psalm of thanksgiving, and with verse 17 in mind ("Do not let me be put to shame, O LORD, for I call on you; let the wicked be put to shame; let them go dumbfounded to Sheol"), it seems silly that the author would be offering his soul up to God. Instead, it appears he is asking for guardianship over that which animates his body and gives him life.[274] The author of Luke-Acts clearly was not aware of the Psalmist's view, let alone of what Israelites thought about the *ruah* or *nefesh* during the times they wrote their books.

Conclusion

We have a very small difference in beliefs, between the non-belief in existence after death, as the earliest Jews put forward, and the dualist view that early Christians held, continuing on from the Greek school of thought. While later Judaism adopted some of the Greek beliefs as well, the dualist view was one that was held, predominantly, in the Christian world of belief. And even when the authors of the canonical books of the New Testament wrote of the soul, they were often misinterpreting passages from the Hebrew Bible to advocate for their beliefs.

In previous chapters I explored how versions of certain philosophies or views changed over time, but I am not sure that is necessary for this section. Outside of there being a belief in

---

[274]Clifford, "Psalms", *Oxford Annotated*, pg. 797

spirits, and perhaps how spirits interact with the physical world, I am ultimately of the opinion that the concept has, more or less, remained the same. With the acceptance of the Greek philosophical position of dualism in antiquity, belief in a spirit, and spiritual world, has persisted. With a rather vague idea of what a spirit is, however, that has left the interpreter to take the word "spirit" to mean whatever they would like it to mean, or be what it is they would like it to be.

With the conclusion of this section, we can now start to explore these ideas and philosophies from an analytical perspective. Can we agree, philosophically, on what a spirit is and whether it is real? What does science say about the immaterial, and is it possible to have an afterlife with that in mind? What of resurrection? Near-death experiences? These are all questions we shall address in our next section.

Chapter 5: Philosophical Arguments for the Afterlife

To start, we need to get some points clear on what we mean by a soul, or a spirit. As Dr. Shelly Kagan states in his philosophy course on death at Yale, "The question isn't 'is there life after death,' but 'can I survive the death of my body?'"[275] Kagan's question is an important one; asking if there is life after life is like me asking if there is insulin production after my pancreas has stopped working. To answer that, "no". No to both. Very much like how I need to go through an artificial process of injecting insulin into my body in order to remain healthy, if an individual's body no longer has the capacity to sustain life, they require life support, in the form of various types of medical equipment, like defibrillators and pacemakers, ventilators, and dialysis machines. For these reasons, among many, keeping a person alive, even if that means doing so on an artificial level, has blurred the line as to when life ends and death takes over.[276]

What, then, is death? According to the 2012 Farlex *Medical Dictionary for the Health Professions and Nursing*, death is "the irreversible cessation of life." It seems fairly straight-forward. Though I may have experienced death, to some small degree, I

---

[275]Kagan, Shelly, *Death: the Nature of Persons: Dualism vs. Physicalism - Lecture 2 Transcript*, Yale Open Courses, January 18, 2007
[276]Singh, Maanvi, "Why Hospitals and Families Still Struggle to Define Death", *NPR*, January 10, 2014, retrieved April 24, 2015, http://www.npr.org/blogs/health/2014/01/10/261391130/why-hospitals-and-families-still-struggle-to-define-death

did not remain dead when my heart stopped so many years ago. Consequently, if we apply this medical definition to what happened with Jesus, Lazarus, or any other figure in the Bible, assuming the people had actually died, then they did not really *die*, as if they had they would have remained dead. Or, at least, if we ignore the writing of Paul, and we focus on the physical resurrection that Luke puts forth, we can correctly assume Jesus did not, in fact, die.

When we consider the idea of life, in a philosophical sense, there are several points to consider. First is the monist view. In so many words, monism is the view that all things derive from a single reality or substance. [277] This view means, in this conversation, that humans are bodies and only bodies. It could also be argued that, given what we know on an astrological and chemical level, all matter is made of the same thing: atoms.[278] So, on a physical level, monism seems to be a sound principle of thought.

On the opposite end of the spectrum is a notion called idealism. Idealism is the thought that, though we see, hear, smell, taste, and touch things that have the sensation of being real, physical objects, it is all an illusion created by our minds. In other words, reality is not *real*.[279] This concept is presented because, in some circles, the words "soul" and "mind," or

---

[277] Cross, F.L., Livingstone, E.A., "monism", *the Oxford Dictionary of the Christian Church*, Oxford University Press, New York, NY, 1974

[278] Barker, G.F., "Divisions of Matter", *A textbook of elementary chemistry: theoretical and inorganic*, Scholarly Publishing Office, University of Michigan Library, 2005, pg. 2

[279] Robinson, Daniel Sommer, "idealism", *Encyclopedia Britannica,* 2015, retrieved April 24, 2015, http://www.britannica.com/EBchecked/topic/281802/idealism

consciousness, are synonymous. People like Deepak Chopra advocate that, while not necessarily synonymous according to their personal philosophies, they are contained within the same immaterial aspect of your body.[280] I know that does not coincide with the idealist perspective, mostly because the view is that there is no body whatsoever, but it does demonstrate the point that people view the soul and the mind as being one thing — or at least as being aligned with one another.

In between these two concepts is one that we have touched on in previous sections: dualism. Dualism is the idea that there are two sides to the world; it can refer to good and evil, or God and Satan for our purposes in the Christian world of morals and philosophy. Some Christian dualists have even argued that free will creates a dualism that separates his creation, or humanity, from him.[281] In Christian theology, and philosophy, this also means that there is a dualistic side of existence. This is one that includes both the physical body, as well as the spiritual ether of the soul or mind. It is the metaphysical understanding of the non-physical part of what believers think is our being.[282]

Arguments for the Soul

Rabbi Adam Jacobs, writing for Huffington Post in 2011, takes arguments for consciousness, quote-mines experts in the fields of philosophy and science saying "Science's biggest mystery is the nature of consciousness," and falsely concludes that this

---

[280]"Deepak Chopra: Your Soul/Consciousness is in your Body" by NewRealities, November 4, 2009, retrieved April 24, 2015, https://www.youtube.com/watch?v=es2JOsBs1Ys
[281]Rouner, Leroy, *the Westminster Dictionary of Christian Theology*, John Knox Press, Louisville, KY, 1983, pg. 166
[282]Kagan, *Death: the nature of persons*, pg. 6-7

means the human body has a soul.[283] Ignoring, for now, that this is purely a "god-of-the-gaps" argument, this is a real question that needs to be considered. *Is our consciousness evidence of a soul?*

No. Of course it is not evidence for the soul. If we were to imagine that the brain is a physical computer, consciousness would simply be a function, or a program, that the computer could run. It is the same idea when we discuss consciousness: it is a function, and not a physical, tangible item that we can see, feel, or hear. A person can be conscious of their surroundings. The temperature, sensations of clothes against their body, sounds of traffic or voices, perhaps tasting and feeling a cigarette between their lips, or a sip of a fresh cup of coffee. While writing, I am conscious of the sounds of my daughter eating cereal, the feeling of my wedding band on my finger, and the hunger that causes my stomach to groan as dinner time approaches. This is consciousness; it is not an object, it has no weight, it has no volume. It is merely a function.

Shelly Kagan uses an excellent comparison for this during his lecture in his philosophy class, which I will attempt to replicate here. Imagine, if you will, a set of lips on a person's face. Imagine, now, that the corners of the lips move up to form a smile. Perhaps it is a thin smile; it is tight-lipped, forced, one you could see given as a polite attempt to acknowledge someone without exerting enthusiasm. Or maybe it's a wide smile, one showing off the teeth of the smiler, bedazzled and exciting, displaying pure joy and warmth to the onlooker. Easy to imagine, right?

---

[283]Jacobs, Rabbi Adam, "A Rational Argument for the Existence of the Human Soul", *Huffington Post Religion*, August 10, 2011, retrieved April 24, 2015, http://www.huffingtonpost.com/rabbi-adam-jacobs/rational-argument-human-soul_b_920558.html

Now, try and imagine a smile without a mouth. No lips, teeth, or gums, not a single part of the face. If this task proves difficult, that is because what you are imagining, or attempting to, is a function of the mouth. A smile is not a thing, but an operation that is performed by a physical part of a person's face. Similarly, consciousness, mindfulness, awareness is a function of the human mind.[284] Similar to chewing for the teeth, digestion for the stomach, or oxygen supply for the lungs, these are all functions that the body performs, but not something that is separate, or independent, from these organs.

A counter to this position is something known as the Cartesian argument, as proposed by Renee Descartes. The scenario, if you will, plays out something like this: Imagine you have woken up one morning and head to the bathroom. As you are, very groggily, rubbing your eyes, thinking of your plans for the day, you flip on the lights and look in the mirror to realize...you are not there. You see your shower, the towel rack, a window; whatever would normally be obstructed from your view with your body in the way. Perhaps you think that maybe all those vampire movies and fantasies you have heard about have come true, except, when you look at your body, you cannot see it still. Your physical body is completely absent from your sight.[285] The whole point of this scenario, as the dualist Descartes intended, was to be able to envision the self, the consciousness or the soul, without the physical body. It is a

[284]Kagan, Shelly, *Death: Arguments for the existence of the soul, Part 1 - Lecture 3*, January 23, 2007, Yale Open Course, pg. 4
[285]Lokhorst, Gert-Jan, "Descartes and the Pineal Gland", *Stanford Encyclopedia of Philosophy*, published April 25, 2005, revised September 18, 2013, accessed April 24, 2015, http://plato.stanford.edu/entries/pineal-gland/

clever argument, but it does not help to make the point that there is a soul.

A perfect example of why it does not work to prove the soul is the Cartesian rebuttal of the morning and evening stars. The evening star is the first celestial body, or light, that is seen in the sky as the sun sets. Likewise, the morning star is the last celestial body of the evening that we see as the sun rises. Now, can you imagine one without the other? It seems a little silly to ask, but the answer should be "of course!" Well, the reason this question is important to ask when considering what we have previously discussed is because the evening and morning star are the same thing! They are both the planet Venus.[286] So, to conceive of one without the other is ridiculous. One does not exist without the other. And so the same can be said of Descartes' argument that there is nothing but an immaterial being.[287]

Building off of this idea, we can infer that the fact that someone can imagine a concept, or scenario, does not make it necessarily real. Just because we can fathom the idea of not being seen in the mirror does not mean someone is capable of being transparent when actually placed in front of one. Just because we think up unicorns, leprechauns, or vehicles that can transform into large, anthropomorphic, autonomous fighting machines, does not mean that they do exist. So, regardless of

---

[286]Cain, Fraser, "Venus, the Morning Star and Evening Star", *Universe Today*, December 19, 2008, retrieved April 24, 2015,
http://www.universetoday.com/22570/venus-the-morning-star/
[287]Siewert, Charles, "Consciousness and Intentionality", *Stanford Encyclopedia of Philosophy*, June 22, 2002, revised December 23, 2006, accessed April 24, 2015,
http://plato.stanford.edu/entries/consciousness-intentionality/

what we can imagine, imagination does not require a feasible, let alone actual, scenario or object.

Another argument for the soul is the argument from free will. Free will says, when it comes to the dualistic choices of right and wrong (ignoring the gray area in such circumstances), each person has a choice not determined by the god of their faith. [288] While considering the concept of free will, in this regard, we must also take into consideration the concept of determinism. Determinism is "the belief that all events are caused by things that happened before them."[289] This area of philosophy argues that, regardless of what one may consciously think and observe, they have no control over their actions because they are determined by all actions prior to the decisions they make. So, the extra cookie you had before dinner, the nasty remark you made toward the person who cut you off in traffic, and the candy bar you shoplifted as a child, were all predetermined. So there is no sense in being upset over it, right? If you are determined to commit a horrendous act like murder due to your genetics and experiences, then you are determined to be placed in a prison system built to protect society from such violent offenders.

Now, what we need to look at is how the natural world around us functions to understand what this means. What becomes obvious, upon close inspection, is that there are deterministic laws of physics. When circumstances are not fully

---

[288]Tooley, Michael, "the Problem of Evil", *Stanford Encyclopedia of Philosophy*, September 16, 2002, revised March 3, 2015, accessed April 24, 2015, http://plato.stanford.edu/entries/evil/

[289]"Determinism", *Merriam-Webster Dictionary Online*, 2015, accessed April 24, 2015, http://www.merriam-webster.com/dictionary/determinism

known, and outcomes are based on probability and predictability, there is still determinism at play but our best current perspective is probabilistic. On the quantum level, if we look at radioactive atoms, we see that these atoms have an 80% chance of decaying — most will, but some do not. Are we able to tell, specifically, which ones? No. Do we know why? No. However, time and again, when we witness radioactive atoms, the majority, 80%, will decay, and a small portion will not. So the laws of physics are deterministic, even if from probabilistic causes.[290]

However, on the other side of this, high-information objects, like DNA, are low on the probability scale, as they are determined by the parents contributing the egg and sperm. It was determined, in other words, by the DNA that my parents contributed to my conception that I would have brown hair and eyes and have diabetes and a heart condition. And so, taking this microcosm and expanding it, civilization is a thing that is of low-probability; there were more deterministic factors being considered than probabilistic.[291]

Let us take, for a brief example, the idea of flipping a coin. Using an American quarter, we see that we have a "heads" side and a "tails" side. Our view is that, when the coin flips in the air, we have a 50% chance of the coin landing on either side because we only have two. However, the laws of physics have determined that by the velocity, spin, and position of the coin at launch, it is determined to land on a particular side. Even if there

[290]Kagan, *Death: Arguments for the existence of the soul, Part III: Free will and near-death experiences, Lecture 5 Transcript*, Yale Open Course, January 30, 2007, pg. 6-7
[291]Stonier, Tom, *Information and Meaning: An Evolutionary Perspective*, Springer Science and Media, New York, NY, 1997, pg. 96-99

were a machine that could accurately toss the coin in the air to make the toss a more probabilistic scenario, there would still be a cause and effect for the end results. Free will would result in the coin landing on a side that was not thought of as an option: to land on its side, or to have the face of Charlie Brown rather than George Washington staring up at us. As Sam Harris details in his book Free Will, "I just drank a glass of water and feel absolutely at peace with the decision to do so. I was thirsty, and drinking water is fully congruent with my vision of who I want to be when in need of a drink…Why didn't I decide to drink a glass of juice? The thought never occurred to me. Am I free to do *that which does not occur to me to do*? Of course not."[292]

My point in this is to demonstrate that, even in probabilistic scenarios with physics on the quantum level, there are deterministic elements that guide the process. In other words, free will is not a rational option, nor is it truly a thing. We carry the illusion of free will since we likely make decisions in our day without coercion of some type, but our decisions, as are all aspects of the physical world, are deterministic. Even in scenarios that are probabilistic, they are very likely being caused by a deterministic factor, even if we do not know at present what that factor may be.

In Plato's *Phaedo*, there is an assumption about the cycle of life. Plato argues that those who have life will eventually die, but then those who die must eventually come back to life. As the living experience death, so do the dead experience birth.[293] Ergo, the "soul" experiences a sort of recycling. From a physics

---

[292]Harris, Sam, *Free Will*, Free Press, New York, NY, 2012, pg. 19
[293]Plato, *Phaedo*, translated by Bejamin Jowett, 71c-d, pg 84 of 171, iBooks edition

perspective, in the classical sense, this might make sense, as the conservation of mass principle dictates that mass cannot be destroyed or created. The only problems are, firstly, this principle applies to a closed system, which our universe is not. And secondly, the soul is assumed to be an immaterial object, so this rule does not apply.[294]

On the quantum level, electrons and positrons are often annihilated in order to create photons, something that is *not always* considered matter. So, it can be argued, that matter *can* in fact be destroyed, or at least become something that is also considered non-matter. Photons also happen to appear out of a vacuum; in other words, there is no real "creation" of photons, they simply become.[295] This is an argument, at least, for the idea that matter can come into existence without a cause — something from nothing.

Despite all of this, even if we do consider matter, or atoms, as having always existed and never having been created before us or destroyed after, it is unlikely, and nearly impossible, to prove that we can demonstrate that anything like a soul existed before us. As an example, we could state that atoms from our left hand came from a different star from our right hand, as

---

[294]Benson, Tom, editor, "Conservation of Mass", *NASA Glenn Research Center*, June 12, 2014, accessed April 25, 2015,
http://www.grc.nasa.gov/WWW/k-12/airplane/mass.html
[295]Kornreich, Dave, "How are photons created and destroyed?", *Ask an Astronomer*, Cornell University, 2015, accessed April 25, 2015,
http://curious.astro.cornell.edu/about-us/137-physics/general-physics/particles-and-quantum-physics/805-how-are-photons-created-and-destroyed-advanced

Lawrence Krauss has so eloquently put it. [296] However, we cannot demonstrate that our hands were perfectly formed, on another human, in another dimension, or in an ethereal realm, prior to our existence. And we also cannot demonstrate that a soul, an allegedly *immaterial* object, could exist, or is part of our existence today, or will be a continued part of our existence after our mortal bodies become lifeless. The ability to experience our existence prior to our birth is just as likely to be experienced afterwards.

Another argument Plato uses in *Phaedo* is that, if we can remember, or recollect, an item perfectly, we must have known it as such prior to a certain circumstance. If I may try my best to give an example: imagine you have a round dinner plate in front of you. Perhaps this is a plate you have only had for a few months; perhaps it is a family heirloom. Regardless of whether it is brand new or not, we can agree that it was made with human hands and, given what is available to us, it is not a perfect object. While it may have the appearance of being perfectly round, we know it cannot be. Once we zoom in to the surface of the edge of the plate, we may see dings, bumps, small craters, etc. As another example, if we look at what the *World Pool-Billiard Association Tournament Table and Equipment Specifications* are, we can see, if we overlook the shape, the surface of the earth, if shrunk to the size of a billiard ball, would more than meet the

---

specifications to be usable in a game. That is right: the earth is, in fact, smoother than a pool ball.[297]

In either case, we can reasonably conclude that, though they may appear perfect on a smaller model, they are anything but. Plato argues that, though we are not able to actually see perfection, we must have experienced it at some time. And when would we have experienced perfection, since we live in an imperfect world? His reasoning is that we experienced it in the life before this one, in the ether, so we must have souls that experienced perfection.[298] Plato equates this to memories of people we know and have had experiences with. My wife is presently not in the room with me, but I have memories of her, so that explains the reality of my belief that she is, in fact, alive and well and not a made-up person. Ignoring that my wife is a living, tangible being for whom I have photos and videos, a birth and marriage certificate, love notes written from her, and so on, it almost seems to make sense. I remember it, so why would it not be true?

The problem, first, is that our memory is incredibly faulty. Dr. Daniel Schacter, a Harvard University psychology professor that specializes in human memory and amnesia, says problems arise in memory from different points. People tend to place their own reactions or feelings in to a memory, which tends to alter how they perceive it. And when a person recalls a memory, it is like pulling out a document in a storm with debris flying around. It is not simply an act of pulling out the document and placing it back in the folder once the memory has served its purpose; it

---

[297]"Proof that the Earth is smoother than a billiard ball", from Curiouser.co.uk, 2001, accessed April 26, 2015, http://www.curiouser.co.uk/facts/smooth_earth.htm
[298]Plato, *Phaedo*, pg. 93

can be influenced by outside factors, like emotions, when the memory is recalled and then placed back where it was found. "When you recall a memory," Schacter says, "it is not simply read out, you have to store and consolidate [stabilize] it again."[299]

More than that, you might not be able to recall every single aspect of a particular moment, because your brain might not deem it worthy to be remembered. When you experience something, your hippocampus, along with the frontal cortex, analyzes all the sensory input from an experience — be it meeting the person you fall in love with, the birth of a child, your first taste of your favorite food, or anything else. If certain stimuli are deemed worthy of being remembered, they are placed in various parts of the brain, as there is not a solitary section responsible for our memory, but a multi-layered, or multi-sectional, approach to recollecting events. The dendrites of the brain, the part responsible for receiving the electrical impulses called synapses, end up receiving more than 100 trillion synapses during events that become memories.[300]

Of course, the problem is that this is not a perfect process. The brain is malleable, and wiring within the brain changes frequently. With each new experience, the brain rewires itself in attempts to make your memory better. The example given in Dr. Richard C. Mohs' article "How Human Memory Works," and

---

[299]Parry, Wynn, "Mystery of Memory: Why it's Not Perfect", *Live Science*, November 16, 2012, accessed April 26, 2015, http://www.livescience.com/24836-mystery-memory-recall.html
[300]Mohs, Richard C., "How Human Memory Works", *How Stuff Works*, March 8, 2007, accessed April 26, 2015, http://science.howstuffworks.com/life/inside-the-mind/human-brain/human-memory.htm

one that I love as a musician, states that, as a musician practices a piece of music over and over, it becomes less difficult to practice, as the same synapses happen over and over in the same pattern. The musician will find the music, over time, easier to play and will make fewer mistakes. But, if the musician stops practicing for several weeks, the brain rewires itself and, when the musician goes back to work on it, it is more difficult to play than when they had been practicing it continuously.[301]

So, it is easy to see why it is so hard to remember things. Part of it, as we have discussed, is that our brain is constantly reshaping itself to be able to remember the most out of experiences that it values as worthy of retention. Some of it is the experiences we go through, and how newer ones change or shift the brain's structure, and some of it is repetition. Yet we forget things because, among other reasons, we simply do not focus enough to allow our hippocampus and frontal cortex to analyze and consider enough of the stimuli — a minimal, or distracted, experience, in other words, will likely be forgotten. Or, perhaps, it is just difficult to remember at that time. Maybe there was a mismatch with your attempt to retrieve the memory, which is why we have things like the very scientifically labelled "brain fart."[302]

All of this is to make a point: the human memory is very flawed. When DNA was finally used and established as capable of identifying perpetrators of a crime, nearly 78% of the US' first 130 convictions were overturned.[303] Prior to physical evidence, with the use of science in genetic identification, eyewitness

---

[301]Ibid.

[302]Ibid.

[303]Stambor, Zak, "How reliable is eyewitness testimony?", *American Psychological Association*, April 2006, vol. 37, number 4, pg. 26

testimony was the best that we had. And that shows to be incredibly faulty and problematic, especially when a person's freedom is at stake. So, with science continuing to demonstrate that our memory is flawed, at best, how can we reasonably take Plato's word that memory of a perfect, or equal, object means it comes from an earlier experience prior to our birth? That aside, research has determined that the area of the brain responsible for helping us develop memory, or at least long-term memory, the frontal lobe, does not start to develop and maintain memory until eight or nine months of age, according to Harvard psychologist Jerome Kagan.[304] Very much like the concept of consciousness, it seems unlikely to experience any sort of memory prior to this stage as memory is clearly a function of a developed brain, not a spiritual experience.

Beyond that, this goes back to the Cartesian argument from before. Just because I can imagine an object perfectly does not mean one exists. It's similar to imagining a theme park full of dinosaurs, or witches acting as prophets to the king's general — just because I can envision it does not make it a reality.

Even if we can prove that a soul is likely, which I feel I have demonstrated is philosophically unlikely, we have an equally difficult task of proving the soul is immortal. A premise is set up in *Phaedo* that suggests that, because the soul is immaterial and invisible, it cannot be destroyed. This depends on the assumption that a soul *does* exist, but we will permit, for a moment, the possibility that one does to continue this argument.

---

[304]Onion, Amanda, "When Do Babies Develop Memories?", *ABC News*, 2015, accessed April 26, 2015, http://abcnews.go.com/Technology/story?id=97848

One of the men in the discussion says that invisible things can be destroyed. What is it, specifically? Harmony. If someone has a harp, he rationalizes, and they are capable of making beautiful music with it, and someone takes a weapon, or blunt object, and hacks away at it while the music is being played, they have, thus, destroyed harmony, an invisible thing.[305]

What is even more telling in this scenario is that, in order to destroy that which was invisible, it was necessary to destroy the physical, tangible object that it depended upon for its existence. Radio waves, by comparison, are invisible things that carry radio, television, and cellular phone signals. They are electromagnetic radiation and, without the proper tools, cannot be detected or interpreted by the human body's senses. This takes it a step further from the argument in *Phaedo* rather than just an invisible thing, we have something that is nearly undetectable. These waves can be interrupted, or blocked, by means of diffraction or objects that conduct electricity. It does, admittedly, depend on the frequency, but diffraction is capable of stopping the signals.[306] And the source of the signals, the transmitter, could also be destroyed, or shut off, thus ending the waves. Again, this is a counterargument that demonstrates the reliance on another object to ensure function of a non-tangible thing.

A Philosophical Argument for Resurrection

Can we rightfully argue, in spite of the philosophical support for the position that there is no possibility of a soul, that

---

[305] Plato, *Phaedo*, pg. 123-130
[306] "Are Radio Waves Blocked?", *InnovateUs*, 2013, accessed April 27, 2015, http://www.innovateus.net/science/how-are-radio-waves-blocked

resurrection could happen? Could we, once we finally face our untimely death, come back to life with our personality, minds, experiences, and all else intact?

We have to face facts that, first, the body decays. Once a person dies, the body starts to decompose and fall apart; our atoms are released back into the cosmos and become a part of life in some other respect (more on that when we get to the section on science). So, can those atoms, hypothetically, come back together to reform you and grant you new life after death?

Well, no; no they cannot. If we take a similar example, cloning, we see that clones will never be 100% exact copies of the people they are cloned from. They could, potentially, have the exact same DNA as the person whose genetics they share, but they lack not only experiences, but the intelligence, ethics, philosophies, and the very same consciousness or personality of the person from whom they were cloned.[307] If we cloned Albert Einstein, as an example, there is no guarantee that his clone would grow up and have an equally great scientific mind. This is due, largely, to the environment the person grows up in. Perhaps this new Einstein would grow up to advance quantum mechanics, something the historical Einstein struggled to accept and understand.[308]

It is likened to the concept of teleportation, as one might see in the science fiction world of works like Star Trek. The idea

---

[307]"Clones aren't exact copies", *Info Please*, Pearson Education, 2007, accessed April 27, 2015,
http://www.infoplease.com/ipa/A0193005.html
[308]Reid, Margaret, "Einstein vs quantum mechanics, and why he'd be a convert today", Phys.org, June 13, 2014, accessed April 27, 2015, http://phys.org/news/2014-06-einstein-quantum-mechanics-hed-today.html

seems very interesting and would be thrilling to try, at least in theory. If you have seen the Mel Brooks movie *SpaceBalls*, you might also see why it is such a bad idea ("Why didn't anyone tell me it was so big?!"). The very hard truth of the matter, when taking physics into account, is that, in order for teleportation to work, it would necessitate completely destroying your body, taking it apart atom-by-atom, and then reassembling it together at another location.

One option for this to function, still with its limitations, is, according to MIT physicist Edward Farhi, quantum teleportation. This would require "particles to be sent ahead of time to the location you want to teleport to... [but] even quantum teleportation takes time; the signal that carries the information used to reconstruct you cannot move faster than the speed of light." While Farhi does admit that "the person at point B should have exactly the same thoughts and memories" as the person who left point A, he also says, in the same line, that they are destroyed, initially, before they are reassembled.[309]

Shelly Kagan addresses this problem in another one of his lectures. He introduces an idea put forward by Peter van Inwagen — a metaphysicist at Notre Dame. Suppose a child in your house, their relationship to you is at your discretion, builds a tower out of blocks and goes to sleep, either for a nap or for the night. While they are asleep, you take careful, considerate notes to map out how the tower is structured. Once you do that, you destroy the block tower and rebuild it exactly as the child did it, down to the minutest detail. Once the child awakes, and

---

[309]Shiga, David, "Teleportation: Fact or fiction?", *New Scientist Space Blog*, January 17, 2008, accessed April 27, 2015,
http://www.newscientist.com/blog/space/2008/01/teleportation-fact-or-fiction.html

sees the block tower, is he or she rightfully able to tell people "This is the block tower I built"? While they may not realize it, as it looks absolutely identical to the one that they built, it is *not* the one they built, but is in fact the one that *you* have built. It is modeled after the one the child made, but it is not the same one.[310]

Likewise, if I purchase an old Nintendo 64 that does not function, and am able to find replacement parts and put it back in working order, the original owner, perhaps noticing a blemish or sticker or detail that they were familiar with on the original system, might say, "Hey, this is my old Nintendo!" But we have to ask, is it really? In this instance, I agree that there are some differences to the previous example and comparing it to teleportation. Still, if we argue that something is destroyed and then placed back together, is it the same thing? Is it still my friend's Nintendo that I put back together in working order? Is it the child's block tower that he or she built, when you are the one that disassembled and reassembled it? Is it the same person who is destroyed in the transmitting teleporter that then is put (back) together in the receiving teleporter?

Now, this is all to make a point about the resurrection. Resurrection, as seen in the study of the Hebrew Bible and New Testament, is the belief that either 1) a spiritual resurrection could occur, which seems unlikely given our discussion about the soul. Or 2) physical resurrection, which, as we have just gone over, seems to really imply that we would not be ourselves, is a legitimate phenomenon. Forget how the resurrection might happen; it is as much a hypothetical as teleportation is. What

---

[310]Kagan, Shelly, *Death: Personal identity, Part II: The body theory and the personality theory - Lecture 11 Transcript*, February 20, 2007, pg. 7

matters is we are talking about the destruction of one body and creation of a new one. While I do not deny processes like the deterioration of the body over time, and even death, I even accept there are ways to improve our body and make it better — be it through education, self-discovery, health, nutrition, or exercise. But to completely dismantle the body and create a new one is not resurrection; it is cloning, at best, with teleportation as a close alternative. And it is questionable, in both instances, whether the being that comes from such a thing is, in fact, the same person who was initially destroyed or who died.

We can, rest assured, not only put aside the notion that our bodies can come back from the dead, but we can also put to bed any discussion or argument encompassing the idea of a resurrection of our current, or a renewed, body, as many have argued. [311] What stands to reason, on both scientific and philosophical grounds, is that the body, in the highly hypothetical circumstance where physical bodies could come back from the dead, would not be your own. It would be a brand new creation that would not be you.

Body and Mind

If we take a physicalist perspective, and I consider this to be my own view, we still have an issue we need to work out. If our lives on this planet are the only lives we get, when do our lives cease? Is it when we stop breathing? Our pulse stops? Our minds stop functioning? Our personality ceases to be? Or is it when our bodies decay and are no longer, physically, in front of us?

---

[311] Hitchens, Christopher, *god is not Great: How Religion Poisons Everything*, Twelve Books, New York, NY, 2007, pg. 143

So, the first idea we are presented with is the idea that the body is the person. By this, I mean, if a person's physical body is present and can be sensed by touch, smell, vision, etc., then the person is alive. The person exists. It is a rather double-edged sword, however, because even if a person no longer has vital signs, what doctors would typically use to determine if there is life in a body, they still exist. Their body is still present; they just exist as a lifeless body.

It can be argued, on a smaller scale, that even if the body changes, that person is still who they are and have not ceased to live. I had an internal pacemaker/defibrillator implanted in my body when I had my heart attack, altering my body permanently. Did that mean I stopped existing at age 14? Of course not! When Aron Ralston, the hiker who had his arm caught under a boulder and had the movie *127 Hours* made about him, amputated his arm himself, did he die when he did so? No, he did not die, despite altering his body in a severe way, for the rest of his life. In fact, in this case, we know he ended up preserving his life because he disfigured his body.

Let us set up a hypothetical situation, as modern science is not yet at this level, to talk about the body as the proof of existence. Suppose there is an auto accident involving two women, we will call them Jane and Sally, and despite the doctors' best efforts they cannot revive Jane as her brain has been too badly damaged. Sally, however, while she has irreparable damage done that makes her bound to a wheel chair with limited mobility, her brain is immaculate — completely free of harm. If they were to take Sally's brain, and place it in the head of Jane, and assuming there are no complications with our semi-futuristic surgery, who would wake up? Would it be Jane or Sally?

This question then brings us to our next concept of existence, or the person, as the mind. We have already talked, at length, about how what we determine as a soul, or consciousness or memory, is a product of the mind, or the brain. And it seems to be with good reason. I am who I am because of the experiences I have had, the relationships I have made, and the environment I grew up in. If I had a traumatic head injury, and woke up thinking I was from Mars and insisted on only speaking in a nonsensical language, would I still be me?

Physically, I am the same person. I still have my scars from my surgery as a child, the same eyes, hair, height, fingerprints, and so on, but suddenly I am aware of myself in a completely different way. If this is so, am I still the same man? The one who experienced the same things, believes (or does not believe) the same things, holds the same relationships, and has the same personality? On a more realistic note, if I were to suffer an even worse fate, and be in a vegetative state, am I the same person then? Not only do I have a completely different personality, but I have absolutely *no* personality, and I do nothing beyond blink and breathe, though I may do so with ventilators. So, in this case, am I still alive?

Take, for example, the case of Terri Schiavo. She was a woman in Florida who suffered a massive heart attack and, as a result, did not receive oxygen to her brain, remained in a coma for two months, and then was in a vegetative state for the remainder of her life. Her remaining years, it should be noted, were 15 due to the fighting from both her parents, the state of Florida, and even President George W. Bush against Schiavo's husband, Michael. She had a tiny chance of recovery, which was never seen, and she had even indicated herself (despite her parents' insistence that it would prove contrary to her Roman

Catholic upbringing) that she wanted her feeding tube removed.[312]

Schiavo's doctors attempted, for two years, to restore her abilities to speak and walk, using speech and physical therapy. But, after so long a period with, at best, minimal progress, they changed her diagnosis to a "consistent vegetative state." This means she had, as stated before, little to no chance of recuperating from her condition. Being that she could no longer carry and express the personality she had before, let alone speak, move, or even eat without assistance, was Terri Schiavo the same person as she was before her heart attack?

Schiavo certainly was not dead after her heart attack, but her life was altered to the point that she could not function, and could not live, without any artificial means of sustaining her life. According to the view of the body, she was very much still alive and existed, albeit not independent of life support equipment. Yet her body did not function as it did, prior to the heart attack. Similarly, according to the mind view, her mind was still active, and she could communicate in a very slight way. However, her personality was gone, or at least was not the same one as before. Her mind had been so badly damaged from a lack of oxygen that it was inhibited to an unchangeable degree.

We are now confronted with a curious situation, after reflecting on the Schiavo case. If we follow the mind, and the mind is limited in its capabilities, as it clearly was for Terri Schiavo, and that inhibited her, physically, from being able to care for herself, including needing machines for her continued

---

[312]Greer, George W., Circuit Judge "In re: the guardianship of Theresa Marie Schiavo, Incapacitated", File No. 90-2908GD-003, Florida Sixth Judicial Court, February 11, 2000, pg. 9-10

existence, was Schiavo truly alive? It is a silly question, but it helps us understand the gray area that comes with questions like these. As an example, and a far more common one, when we are asleep at night, or whenever it is we sleep, are we truly alive? It seems just as silly as asking if Schiavo was alive, but it brings up the same line of questions. Are we capable of expressing ideas and emotions, and showing personality when we are asleep? Are we as physically capable of expressing ourselves as when we are awake? When we sleep, we are in an altered state of consciousness and are far less capable of, and responsible for, feelings and movement. During the third and fourth stage of sleep, where we spend the least amount of time while asleep, there is no muscle or eye movement.[313] While there are certainly many benefits to your psyche that you achieve while you sleep, including that it makes you easier to get along with, better at decision making, and better at handling memories that create anxiety,[314] we do not exhibit the same level of awareness as we would while awake. While we dream, we are involved in the dream and not what is going on in the real world. Even when we have lucid dreams, where we are aware of the fact we are dreaming, we are so caught up in our surroundings *within the dream* that we think and are aware on a level that it is not comparable to our awareness of the physical world our bodies

---

[313]"Brain Basics: Understanding Sleep", *National Institute of Neurological Disorders and Stroke*, last updated July 25, 2014, accessed April 29, 2015, http://www.ninds.nih.gov/disorders/brain_basics/understanding_sleep.htm

[314]Gregoire, Carolyn, "5 Amazing THings Your Brain Does While You Sleep", *Huffington Post,* September 8, 2014, accessed April 29, 2015, http://www.huffingtonpost.com/2014/09/28/brain-sleep-n_5863736.html

are in. So, for all intents and purposes, it would appear, for some time while we sleep, that we are not alive, at least according to those that follow the mind.

Perhaps sleep is not the best example, as it is only a temporary end of the function of the body and, at the very least, a small lapse in our awareness of ourselves and our surroundings. However, this then brings up an interesting theological point: if death is a permanent cessation of our bodies and minds, then when God is supposed to have brought the dead back to life, like in Revelation or even in Matthew 27 with all the saints rising up after the crucifixion or even Jesus' own resurrection, were they ever really dead? It would appear that, when we consider this definition of death, the people coming back to life were never really dead but in a prolonged slumber.[315] Until the prophesized day of resurrections comes, and it seems unlikely it ever will, we have already explored enough to know that it is questionable that they would be the same person, let alone that they died to begin with. Perhaps this is why all the groups out there that claim to be capable of bringing the dead back to life, will not do it in front of a skeptical audience. Or, at the very least, why people who know better are turning them away.[316]

A question of the consciousness of an individual is brought up because of the view that consciousness is "proof" of a metaphysical soul. In other words, because we experience the self and the emotions of the self, there must be something more

---

[315]Kagan, Shelly, *Death: The nature of death (cont.); Believing you will die - Lecture 15 Transcript*, Yale Open Courses, March 6, 2007, pg. 2-3
[316]Firma, Terry, "Bible Inspires Ordinary Christians to Raise the Dead, Just Like Jesus. Are You Ready For the Zombie Apocalypse?", *Patheos*, May 25, 2013, accessed April 29, 2015, http://tinyurl.com/qbmbjep

than just the physical body. However, as is the case of Schiavo, consciousness, and perhaps the personality that is exhibited with consciousness, does not a soul make. Our consciousness exists as a way to create awareness of our surroundings, to understand relationships between the self and objects around the self, and how to adapt to surroundings in order to help our genes get passed along.[317]

We also would like to believe that our consciousness is attributed to our physical bodies and, though our bodies may change, the consciousness does not. This concept could not be further from the truth, as we can see consciousness changes in various forms. Strokes can lead to people losing conscious visual perception, people lose consciousness of their present circumstances thanks to Alzheimer's disease, and numerous experiments have demonstrated that changes in neurochemical processes create experiences unique to the individual.[318] In other words, while we would like to believe we remain the same for the duration of our mortal lives, science says something quite contrary to that concept.

Questions of morality, existence, and humanity are not black and white issues. It is difficult to look at a situation where the mind does not function and to say, "Ah, yes, this person no longer has the capability to communicate, show personality, or

---

[317]Andavolu, Krishna, "Sorry Religions, Human Consciousness Is Just a Consequence of Evolution", *Vice*, September 12, 2013, accessed September 21, 2015, http://www.vice.com/read/sorry-religions-human-consciousness-is-just-a-consequence-of-evolution

[318]Shermer, Michael, "What Happens to Consciousness When We Die", *Scientific American*, July 1, 2012, accessed September 21, 2015, http://www.scientificamerican.com/article/what-happens-to-consciousness-when-we-die/

even speak. She must be dead." All Schiavo's vital signs are there; medically, it appears she is alive. At the same time, we see she is using life-support machines to assist her continued existence. What finally ended her life, by the medical definition, was the removal of her feeding tube, after attempts to do that were unsuccessful for 15 years. Physically, it would seem, Schiavo was, or would have been, just as alive as her mind without support.

Instead of looking at this situation as a matter of a corpse that we kept the blood flowing through in order to maintain some sign of brain activity, it may be more considerate, and realistic, to observe it in a more middle-ground arena. Schiavo, as have many others in similar circumstances, had stopped being a person. This is not to be confused with being a human being; nothing changes that. But being in a chronic, vegetative state, as she was, means one loses awareness of the self, even after waking from a coma. She lacked cognitive function but retained the capability to demonstrate a sleep-wake function.[319] By losing both capabilities, of body and mind, Schiavo had become a being that was not herself — or not the "her" who existed prior to the heart attack that caused her to be in the state she was in. So, even though she may have been alive, artificially or otherwise, she was not Terri Schiavo, physically or mentally.

On the other side of the argument, and to help us understand my point better, when do we even begin being a person? Again, this is not to confuse being a person with being a human. This is to understand when our personality, our sense of

---

[319]"Vegetative state", *Gale Medical Encyclopedia*, 2008, accessed April 28, 2015, http://medical-dictionary.thefreedictionary.com/Vegetative+State

self and identity, is formed or created. I was not a person when half of me was an egg in my mother and the other half a sperm in my father. Even when they joined, I still was not suddenly capable of making statements of preference or voicing my opinion, let alone forming cohesive thoughts. Neither was I during my nine months in my mother's womb, or for a long while even after I was born. Up to the eight or nine month mark of an infant's life, they do not even have object permanence — the ability to know an object or person is still there, even if not in sight.[320] I do not mean to bring up issues to dwell on, and these might be more suitable for a debate on abortion and the issue of when life begins, but it helps us to understand the concept of consciousness and when a human body truly becomes a person.[321]

Now, if I lived to be as old as the men purported to have existed in the Hebrew Bible, living for several centuries like Adam did in Genesis, do we assume that I would always be the same person? I can look back at the person I was ten years ago and know that I am nothing like that man. In another decade, I may likely look back at the "me" of this moment, or age, and be sure I am not that person anymore. So, if I live several hundred years, could I be a completely polar opposite to the person I am today? Could I look back and curse my decision to drive a hybrid, write books on theology, and question the existence of the supernatural? That is surely not a person I would look

---

[320]"Psychology glossary: Object permanence", AlleyDog.com, 2015, accessed April 29, 2015,
http://www.alleydog.com/glossary/definition.php?term=Object%20Permanence
[321]Kagan, Shelly, *What Matters (cont.); The nature of death, Part I - Transcript*, Yale Open Courses, March 1, 2007, pg. 14

forward to becoming. But it does not mean I died the moment I embraced SUVs, writing romance novels, or completely ignoring all my education and embracing a creator god and faith. It does mean I am not the same person. But, if my personality changed so much to a point where I lacked one, where I was non-responsive and demonstrated few noticeable changes in behavior aside from being awake and asleep, that would be, truly, the death of who I am.

Likewise, if years down the road I am in a horrible accident and have an arm amputated, or if I meet my father who, having taken a turn towards evil, chops off my hand in a duel, I do not die. If, later, I suffer another tragedy and lose the ability to use my legs and am labeled a paraplegic, I am not dead then either. When I lost the function of my pancreas when I was seven, and was diagnosed with diabetes, I did not die then, though part of my body did (or at least stopped functioning). Yet, if I had such a horrific accident that caused me to lose all capabilities of my body, including communication and the ability to express emotions through body movements or facial expressions, that is a complete change in who I am. I am not capable of expressing who I am or what I am feeling. This is even true if I am completely conscious, similar to how this scenario was dramatized in the April 2015 episode of *Grey's Anatomy* when Patrick Dempsey's character is in a vegetative state after being hit by a car. He is capable of feeling, hearing, sensing, and even narrating how he *should* be cared for by the hospital staff, but is not, outwardly, capable of communicating that to them. In that instance, his character dies. It could be argued he was partially dead prior to his clinical death at the end, as he lacked the ability to express himself physically. And no, I will not apologize for watching *Grey's Anatomy*.

Anyone in the position of someone like Schiavo, or Dempsey's character, is no longer themselves; they lose their awareness, and their personality goes with that too. Instead of continuing on like a broken record about the point, I will simply close this section by stating that the point of the end of our existence is blurry. And, with the advancements in modern medicine, that line becomes ever fuzzier. With movies like Johnny Depp's *Transcendence* bringing up the idea of consciousness without a body, then do we reach true immortality if we ever reach that point? Time, and ethicists, will surely tell. Until then, we shall continue to face the problems, or build them, with the technology and advances we have and new ethical issues that arise with life, and end of life, decisions.

What Do We Want?

These are difficult questions, I understand. There are no easy answers to these, but they are brought up to ask one, very important, question. Philosophically, physically, and theologically, what is it that we are hoping to have when we do have any sort of life?

We have already explored why it seems unlikely that souls exist, at least philosophically. But, for a moment, let us pretend there actually is a sliver of a chance we will experience a life after we stop living the physical, mortal one. Do we want a life like the late Terri Schiavo? Do we wish to experience the world in a way where we only perceive and, perhaps, feel? Do we not desire to continue to read, walk, play with our children, watch and react to sporting events, drive a car? The list goes on, but I can ask the question in a much simpler way: is it enough to have simply a conscious life after we die? Probably not.

Would it then be okay to live a sort of Stephen Hawking-style of life after death? My greatest respects to Dr. Hawking; I mean no ill in using his physical capabilities in my example, but it helps me to demonstrate my question. Is it enough for us, is it what we want, to be able to communicate, think, learn, read, and experience, but with very suppressed mobility? Do we want a life where our personality is there, but is still pretty limited?

We could continue on this path to various degrees, but, ultimately, we are faced with the conclusion that people would likely want complete lucidity with their body movements and ability to express themselves — to express their personality. More than that, because of passages like Matthew 11:5 ("The blind receive sight, the lame walk, those who have leprosy are cleansed, the deaf hear...", though we should probably ignore the tail end of this passage that notes "the dead are raised"), people likely feel that that is what awaits them when they arrive in the afterlife. Of course, that also means they are not aware of what Jesus meant when he spoke about the kingdom of heaven.

I do not think it would be too wild to assume that we all want a life where we have free movement of our bodies, and we all want to maintain a personality and freedom to express that personality the same way we presently do, or would want to. So, the question then becomes, would we have that if there was an afterlife to greet us in the end?

For a moment, I am going to assume, not only that there is an afterlife, but that there is one as taught by the Catholic Church. I use the Catholic Church as it is the faith I really grew up knowing, it is the most subscribed to sect of the Christian faith, and it is what my education in theology focused in. Despite the fact that the Second Vatican Council (1.2.839-848) said that salvation is available to all, it is only through Jesus that it can be received (a clear reference to the Gospel of John 14:6). If we imagine, through some divine miracle, that we, both you the reader and I, are welcomed into the Catholic paradise, is this an afterlife, let alone any type of life, that we would like? I would question the tenets of the faith we would need to adhere to should we be welcomed into the Catholic afterlife.

First, does this mean I cannot take a razor to my face in Heaven, like Leviticus 19:27 says? Will I be automatically ejected because of my tattoos, as Leviticus 19:28 dictates? Will I not be permitted to eat bacon — as Deuteronomy 14:8 declares pigs unclean — unless it is turkey bacon? I do not mind it, but prefer bacon from a pig. Catholicism clearly has no prohibitions against these items, but there are sects of Judaism, Islam, and perhaps even Christianity that do adhere to these rules.

Will I not enjoy the company of my friends who identify as transgendered, transsexual, or homosexual? The Bible does not, in fact, condemn homosexuality,[322] as many have addressed, and as I discuss in my book *What the Bible Really Does (and Doesn't) Say About Sex*.[323] Yet, the Catholic Church has a strong position against homosexuality, transgenderism, and transsexuality. If I am not permitted to enjoy an afterlife with some of my closest friends, some who I consider family, then would I be truly happy?

While I am not proud to put forward this next idea, it is one that is worth mentioning. On a Yahoo Answers forum, someone who was a Christian asked, to paraphrase, what would happen to his non-Christian family when they all died. Could he be happy

---

[322]Shore, John, "the Best Case for the Bible Not Condemning Homosexuality", *Huffington Post*, April 3, 2012, accessed April 28, 2015, http://www.huffingtonpost.com/john-shore/the-best-case-for-the-bible-not-condemning-homosexuality_b_1396345.html

[323]O'Neil, Matthew, *What the Bible Really Says (and Doesn't Say) About Sex: the How, When, Why, and With Whom of Scriptural Prohibitions and Permissions*, Pitchstone Publishers, Durham, NC, 2015

in heaven knowing, or believing, that his family was suffering in hell? The best rated comment stated that God would help him forget his family.[324] Well, if you are made to forget, particularly people who played a huge role in your life and were fundamental in your development as a being, especially your entire family, is that freedom? Is it paradise, let alone heaven? It seems contrary to me, being someone who cares deeply about his family, to be made to forget people suffering for, what is believed to be, an eternity. Further, if we are made to forget something, anything, is that a part of our personality and consciousness that we are willing to give up? If I was offered the opportunity to escape a lifetime of punishment, but I had to willingly, or by force, forget a rather large part of my personal history (I imagine this as a vehement *Eternal Sunshine of the Spotless Mind* kind of concept), it would be dishonest to say it would be an easy choice.

My point in discussing this is as follows: in order to be able to gain entry into heaven, as contemporary believers assume heaven to be the great reward for a faithful life, regardless of their faith, it means a restriction on who they are, as well as how you interact with others, in order to do so. Perhaps as a Protestant, a Muslim, a Buddhist, or even an atheist having been granted access into the heavenly realm, those not familiar with the faith would need to make some drastic changes in order to stay. And given the frequent singing songs and exclamations of praise to God, like in Revelation 14:3, it seems more like submission. It looks like you are brought into a place much like

---

[324] https://answers.yahoo.com/question/index?qid=20100530230052A Awn1CY

modern day North Korea,[325] with thousands making attempts each year to escape.[326] After days, weeks, years, a millennia of constant worship and praise to Yahweh, when would we start looking for a way out, and to what lengths would we go to achieve it?

Heaven, as it may seem, is anything but paradise. Perhaps even to those who believe it to be a real thing.

Conclusion

We run into many deep questions and concerns when we talk about the possibility with the afterlife and the soul. And while we can offer examples as to why they may or may not work, we are not always left with a simple yes or no answer. This is particularly true when we deal with the concept of the body and mind and what it means to be alive. Are we alive if our bodies are still physically here with no mind intact? Are we alive with simple awareness and no personality? Are we alive with limited awareness and mobility? What about with zero mobility and the ability to demonstrate consciousness and personality, the way Dr. Stephen Hawking is? These are all difficult questions, and equally difficult are the answers.

Personally, I am a physicalist in terms of life, but I follow the mind, as Dr. Shelly Kagan would say. I very much am of the opinion that our life is solely one that we live on this planet with nothing to follow once our consciousness fails. If our vital signs

---

[325]Patel, Hasan Salim, "Christopher Hitchens: A Life in Quotes", *Al Jazeera English*, December 16, 2011, accessed September 11, 2015
[326]McKenzie, David, "'Snakehead' gangs offer only escape for North Korea's defectors", *CNN*, November 19, 2014, accessed April 28, 2015, http://www.cnn.com/2014/11/19/world/asia/china-north-korea-defector-escape-mckenzie/

drop, because of what happens naturally or when we unplug any life-sustaining technology that may be keeping us alive, then that is it for me, for any of us.

But our lives are reliant on our bodies as well. For our minds to function we need blood, oxygen, and nutrients to be supplied to the mind; even if the brain is put into another body, it still relies on the body in order to function. Damage the body, and the mind is affected — if not physically, then psychologically for certain. Likewise, if the mind is impacted, then the body, in turn, is as well. It is not a matter of one being predominantly responsible for who we are, but instead each is reliant on the other.

This whole discussion of mind and body is the baseboard for the larger discussion of the afterlife — in regards to souls, to life beyond the death of our bodies and/or minds, and where such a life would take place. If we understand that consciousness is a function, rather than an ethereal entity separate from our physical selves, then it makes no sense to believe in souls. If we do not believe in the soul, then it makes no sense to argue for an afterlife. But if we do permit room for a soul, detectable or otherwise, do we know what kind of life we will have once we pass on to the next world? If it is limited, then what is the sense of having a life after the death of my mind and body? If it is one as explained in the Gospel of Matthew, and we have full lucidity of movement and thought, are we then restricted to how we *should* think? If so, we do not truly have the freedom that our culture would embrace, as different religious dogmas would not permit different actions or beliefs. And if that is the case, then the afterworld would seem rather restrictive and more of a burden than a welcome place. Would someone truly enjoy an eternity (or, really, any period longer than an hour or two) of worship and praise of someone or something? If they were made to enjoy it, as some might argue we would be made to forget the people we love suffering in hell, is it even a reward?

"But," the reader may be thinking, "what of all the science behind it?" Near death and out of body experiences? Visions of angels? Voices? The feelings of people being in the room with you? Well, frankly, these arguments do not hold up to scrutiny as well as believers would like you to think. As Victor Stenger shows, among many other fabulous points, in cases like Near Death Experiences (NDEs as we shall refer to them later), the only similar detail for such accounts across the globe is seeing other beings and being in another realm. All else is dependent on the culture in which the person making the claim grew up.[327] As we shall see, moving in to our next section, other aspects of religion and the afterlife can be explained with science, or even dismissed due to the irregularity in agreement between faiths and cultures.

And now, on to science.

[327]Stenger, Victor J., *God and the Folly of Faith: the Incompatibility of Science and Religion*, Prometheus Books Amherst, NY, 2012, pg. 236-237

Chapter 6: The Science of the Afterlife

What Happens When We Die?

Recapping a bit from our philosophical discussion, the act of dying is the permanent cessation of life from a being. In other words, when the synapses stop firing in the brain, the lungs stop taking in air, the heart stops beating, and there are no signs of consciousness or identity, that is when death occurs. It is a continuous, ongoing, permanent state of (non)being. No Heimlich Maneuver performed, no CPR, no first aid, no life support can change it; the body and mind have ceased to function and there is no turning the switch back on for them. Regardless of how death happens, it has happened and it is permanent.

A person who believes in the afterlife, assuming they have skipped over everything else we have discussed in the book, might come to this section and say "That is not the end! There is still life after death. We have evidence, not just biblical or philosophical, but physical, scientific evidence by well-known researchers and scientists, to demonstrate the plausibility and reality of life beyond death." They may say this believing it to be the absolute truth, but just because someone believes something does not make it true. Empirical, testable, evidence does.

After Life

Reincarnation

I remember many years ago, I put forward an argument that reincarnation seemed unlikely, though I may have said impossible. Reincarnation is the belief that a person's soul has been granted another chance at life in a new body.[328] I remember telling the person with whom I was talking, that reincarnation was unlikely, or impossible, because the people who most often claimed to be reincarnated often did it with easily accessible information on the person they claimed to be. And, very often, it was someone well known and of historical significance. So, of course, it is easy to say you are the reincarnation of someone and have good details about who they were if they have made it into history books, or tabloid magazines. The rebuttal, expletives and name-calling aside, was that I did not know what I was talking about and clearly had not done my research. However, when I did my research, it turned out I was not far from the simple claim I had made.

A Gallup poll taken in 2001 showed that 25% of the population in the United States believed in reincarnation.[329] In 2013, though it saw a three point increase from 2009, the results were relatively the same at 24% of people in the US.[330] And,

---

[328]"Reincarnation", Merrian-Webster.com, Merrian-Webster, 2015, accessed April 30, 2015, http://www.merriam-webster.com/dictionary/reincarnation
[329]Roach, Mary, *Spook: Science Tackles the Afterlife,* W. W. Norton and Co., New York, NY, 2006, Kindle Edition, pg. 34
[330]Shannon-Missal, Larry, "Americans' Belief in God, Miracles, and Heaven Declines", *Harris Interactive* , December 16, 2013, accessed April 30, 2015, http://www.harrisinteractive.com/NewsRoom/HarrisPolls/tabid/447/ctl/ReadCustom%20Default/mid/1508/ArticleId/1353/Default.aspx

157

though it may be believed to a degree that remains relatively unchanged, a belief in an idea does not make it a real thing. What makes such a concept hard to accept, let alone prove, is that it is not something that can be shown in a scientific setting. There is no biological set up for it, as it is the concept of an immaterial thing traveling with no physical or biological make up. So trying to do such a thing with science can prove to be difficult.

One such argument is that of children born with birthmarks resembling types of wounds that the person they claim to have been suffered in a past life. While we do not have a complete understanding of birthmarks, it would be deceitful to say a likely, or probable, explanation is reincarnation. We do know that, often, birthmarks can be a collection of cells or abnormal blood vessels under the skin.[331]

Part of the problem with these claims, such as those from the boy with unilateral microtia (a malformed ear) who claimed to have memories of being a man who had died from a shotgun blast to the right side of his face among others, is that it is pushed forward with pseudoscience like that pushed by Ian Stevenson. His article "Birthmarks and Birth Defects Corresponding to Wounds on Deceased Persons" appeared in the *Journal of Scientific Exploration* (Vol. 7, No. 4, pp. 403-410, 1993).[332] And, while it would seem the scientific community

---

[331]Nordqvist, Christian, "What are birthmarks? What causes birthmarks?", *Medical News Today*, last update September 26, 2014, accessed April 30, 2015, http://www.medicalnewstoday.com/articles/174886.php

[332]http://www.scientificexploration.org/journal/jse_07_4_stevenson.pdf

accepted his views despite the fact that one of the key words in his paper is "paranormal processing," since its publication the scientific community has been very vocal in denouncing the views of Stevenson. It has been noted that there is confirmation bias in his studies, leading questions that are asked of the participants involved in the studies he does, and an overt willingness to believe stories, even those that were exaggerated, by Stevenson.[333] Terrence Hines, a professor of neurology at Pace University in New York, wrote, "In the seemingly most impressive cases Stevenson has reported, the children claiming to be reincarnated knew friends and relatives of the dead individual. The children's knowledge of facts about these individuals is, then, less than conclusive, or completely non-conclusive, evidence for reincarnation."[334]

A similar concept, called "past life regression," is also purported to prove reincarnation. Dr. Brian Weiss, who is an American psychiatrist, is alleged to have talked to many people who have experienced these past lives, including one woman who believes she married a man who was a person with the soul of the son from her previous life.[335] The problem with this, despite what Dr. Weiss might presume, and as we will see time and again, anecdotal evidence is anything but in the scientific

[333]Carroll, Robert Todd, "Ian Stevenson (1918-2007)", *the Skeptics' Dictionary*, last revised December 23, 2013, accessed April 30, 2015, http://www.skepdic.com/stevenson.html
[334]Hines, Terrence, *Pseudoscience and the Paranormal*, Prometheus Books, New York, NY, 2003, pg. 109
[335]Weiss, Brian, *Messages from the Masters: Tapping into the Power of Love*, Grand Central Publishing, New York, NY, 2000, pg. 85

realm. Further, as Dr. Victor Stenger writes, "the plural of anecdote is not 'data.'"[336]

An issue, among many, that arises with this belief is that the method that is performed to determine if someone has had a "past life regression" uses memory as a reliable source of evidence. We have already discussed the issues with memory in a previous section, so there is no need to attempt to address the topic again. But it is important that we note what is used for evidence for those who are "experts" in this field. It has been found that people working in this field also use suggestive, or leading, questions to attempt to guide the individual to answer in a specific way and, in turn (should they be recollecting legitimate memories), distorts the memory or even creates new, false ones.[337] It has also been found, when investigated, that the stories people give of past lives are false because of historical inaccuracies — plagued with modern concepts of historical events influenced by pop-culture and misinformation taken out of popular books.[338]

In cases where it is more culturally common to believe in reincarnation, like in India where 80% of the population practices Hinduism (a practice that has reincarnation as a central tenet of the faith),[339] we are faced with a lot of the same issues as before. Further, when an instance of reincarnation comes up

[336]Stenger, *Folly of Faith*, pg. 235

[337]Shermer, Michael, *The Skeptics Encyclopedia of Pseudoscience, Vol. 1*, ABC-CLIO, Santa Barbara, CA, 2002, pg. 206-207

[338]Carroll, Robert Todd, *the Skeptics Dictionary: A Collection of Strange Beliefs, Amusing Deceptions, and Dangerous Delusions*, John Wiley and Sons, Hoboken, NJ, 2003, pg. 276-277

[339]"Hinduism", *Info Please*, Pearson Education, 2007, accessed May 1, 2015, http://www.infoplease.com/ipa/A0001469.html

in these areas, it is talked about at great length with the person, sometimes even a young child, claiming to have led a life in the past without writing down the original statement of the claim. This leads to exaggeration and filling in gaps with made up stories; and even the villagers in the community can be dishonest and fill in parts of the story for the person making the claim.[340]

A larger clue, and perhaps what should be noted as an important red flag, is that often rich families that are targeted by people. A child of a poor family will make a claim of reincarnation, saying that they used to be a part of a royal, or well-to-do, family, and hope for an offer of an inheritance. A woman once used the excuse of having her body inhabited by a new soul when she was ill. She was not dead, or near death, but she made the claim so she could refuse to sleep with her husband, stating her spouse from a previous life would not approve of it. She did this because, in this culture, divorce has a very negative stigma, so she used this as an opportunity to refuse any sort of romantic, or otherwise, relations with her husband.[341]

I think it is safe to say, all things considered, that reincarnation is not a legitimate phenomenon. Between the false scientific study that goes into it, the falsification of memories, the guidance to "remember" things that never happened, and understanding that, in the culture where it is most popular and practiced, it is often done as means for looking for a monetary gift (or an option to refrain from intimacy), reincarnation is anything but real.

---

[340]Roach, *Spook*, pg. 27
[341]Ibid.

The Soul

If we were to believe in the soul, we would need to think about where, in our body, the soul might be housed. René Descartes, a French philosopher dubbed the father of modern philosophy, thought that the soul was housed in the pineal gland in the brain.[342] We know this gland, today, to regulate melatonin in the brain that affects the sleep patterns in seasonal and circadian rhythms, and studies on rats have suggested it also affects the pituitary gland's secretion of sex hormones.[343]

Prior to this, many claims were made about the soul being housed in the brain, similar to Descartes'. Herophilus, a fourth century BCE Greek physician, thought the brain held the soul in the ventricles. Galen, a second century Greek physician, decided that the brain held the soul as well. But after cutting his neighbors' pigs brains, he decided, unlike Herophilus, that the soul was in the actual substance of the brain.[344]

In the eighteenth century CE, Gigot de la Peyronie, founder of France's Royal Academy of Surgery, wrote a paper titled, "Observations by Which One tries to Discover the Part of the Brain Where the Soul Exercises its Functions." In this paper, he detailed work he did on a sixteen-year-old boy who had suffered a severe head trauma and was in, or went into, a coma. When he performed surgery, Peyronie found an abscess on the corpus callosum in the boy's brain. Today, we know this section of the brain as the fibers between the two hemispheres that help the

---

[342]Roach, *Spook*, pg. 65
[343]Motta, Mariana, Fraschini, F., Martini, L., "Endocrine Effects of Pineal Gland and Melatonin", *Experimental Biology and Medicine*, 1967, accessed May 1, 2015, http://ebm.sagepub.com/content/126/2/431
[344]Roach, *Spook*, pg. 69

left and right sides of the brain communicate. But, when Peyronie drained the abscess, the boy suddenly came out of his coma. It eventually refilled, and the boy slipped back into a coma. Peyronie drained it, and he awoke. So, Peyronie reasoned, the corpus callosum must be the "seat of the soul." However, the sixteen-year-old died, as did subsequent patients who had similar abscesses during trials like this one under Peyronie.[345]

In terms of Descartes' assumption that the soul is housed in the pineal gland, it seems that idea is wrong as well. A condition, known as polymicrogyria, exists where people are born *without* a pineal gland, thanks to a PAX6 mutation.[346] PAX6 is part of a family of genes that not only help cell production during the embryonic stage of development (like those of the eyes, brain, and spinal cord), but they also maintain the function of the normal cells and proteins after birth (including those responsible for our sense of smell).[347] It also appears that, though it is rare for vertebrate animals to be without one, one species is known to not have the pineal gland: the armadillo.[348]

In spite of all the objections that have been presented, and demonstrably shown, that the soul, if one exists, is not located in the brain or anywhere within the body, people have still gone

---

[345]Roach, *Spook*, pg. 70

[346]Mitchell, T. N., Free, S. L., Williamson, K. A., Stevens, J. M., Churchill, A. J., Hanson, I. M., Shorvon, S. D., Moore, A. T., van Heyningen, V. and Sisodiya, S. M., "Polymicrogyria and absence of pineal gland due to PAX6 mutation", *Annals of Neurology*, 2003, 53: 658–663. doi: 10.1002/ana.10576

[347]"PAX6", *Genetics Home Research*, April 28. 2015, accessed May 1, 2015, http://ghr.nlm.nih.gov/gene/PAX6

[348]Yu, Hing-Sing, and Reiter, Russell J., *Melatonin: Biosynthesis, Physiological Effects, and Clinical Applications,* CRC Press, Boca Raton, FL, 1992, pg. 221

out of their way to demonstrate that one exists. In the case of a Dr. Duncan MacDougall, a physician in Haverhill, MA, he made efforts to demonstrate the existence of a soul based on a loss of mass when people died. As he wrote, "It is unthinkable that personality and consciousness can be attributes of that which does not occupy space." He made this attempt by putting a Fairbanks scale, one used for manufacturing purposes (the weighing of larger objects, or large quantities), in a home for people who were in the later stages of tuberculosis and were assumed to be on the road to dying. He then, after receiving consent in writing, placed people on the scale as they were dying to attempt and measure the weight loss, if any, once they died.[349]

MacDougall thought he received confirmation of this. On April 10, 1901, at 5:30 PM, he and two others witnessed the scale drop three-quarters of an ounce, or 21 grams. While he considered it a huge success, there were numerous criticisms and questions that arose. One was, as I was inclined to believe, that upon the expiration of a body, the bowels and bladder tend to void their contents. Not so, said MacDougall. Even if or when the body emptied itself of any waste, it would have, or did, stay on the scale. Others assumed that the 21 grams was the last breath leaving the body, but MacDougall demonstrated that, even if breathing heavily in and out, there was no change in the weight.[350]

For each criticism lobbed at MacDougall, he appeared to have the correct response in mind. And it would seem he had a valid point, but his theory, and his results, were still incredibly flawed. Despite the fact that this body had lost weight at the

---

[349]Roach, *Spook*, pg. 80
[350]Roach, *Spook*, 81-82

supposed moment of death, it was the only one that presented these results. There were only six bodies used in the study; the first was the only one that lost, and kept off, the weight. Two were not usable due to technical difficulties, one lost half an ounce, but then gained a full ounce minutes later, one was reported to have lost half an ounce, but it was due to someone nudging the scale when a stethoscope was used to determine that the individual had died.[351] That then raises the question, how did they know the individuals were dead without using a stethoscope? And would that not have contributed to the weight gain or loss in the process? Authorities eventually put a stop to MacDougall, who spent the rest of his medical career working with euthanizing dogs. None of which showed any sign of dropping weight at death.[352] Needless to say, as Dr. Robert L. Park has written, MacDougall's findings "are not regarded today as having any scientific merit."[353]

Subsequent experiments have taken place to attempt to prove that there is matter and weight to the soul, including one by Harry Laverne Twining, who was a physics teacher at Los Angeles' Polytechnic. He closed live mice inside a test tube, using a Bunsen burner to close the end, and found no change. He attempted closing the tubes with corks, flashes with parafinned corks, also with no change. When he attempted cyanide, he found a one to two milligram difference. This may have to do with why cyanide was viewed as a cruel and unusual

---

[351]Kruszelnicki, Karl, *Great Mythconceptions: the Science Behind the Myths*, Andrews McMeel Publishing, Kansas City, MO, 2006, pg. 200-202

[352]Roach, *Spook*, pg. 89

[353]Park, Robert L., *Superstition: Belief in the Age of Science*, Princeton University Press, Princeton, NJ, 2009. pg. 90

form of execution — as the death was deemed aerobic. It entailed panic, seizures, violent head extensions, retching and excessive salivating (which may have contributed to the weight change).[354] Both experiments, on mice and dogs, provided us with no conclusion that, if a soul existed, it had any weight.

In 1998, using the methods and information provided by MacDougall (which was very likely the first mistake made), Donald Gilbert Carpenter wrote a book called *Physically Weighing the Soul* and decided the ratio of soul weight, from humans to dogs, is 1 to 140. So, he puts the weight of a dog's soul at 1 gram and determines that it would be so light that modern scales would not be able to detect it. He makes a similar argument for mice — being that they are much smaller, by ratio so would the weight of their soul. However, if you want to know the weight of Jesus' soul, he has an answer for that too: 364 grams, nearly a full pound. And he also said leprechauns are likely "disincarnate humans" and used his ratio findings to determine their weight.[355] I really wish that was a joke, but it is very real. Someone not only wasted their time to figure out how bad science could be used to try and weigh something for which there was no proof, but then used the same ratio to weigh a non-existent, immaterial thing on a non-existent, known mythological character. Sometimes, truth truly is stranger than fiction.

Despite all the study gone into a soul having mass, and by proxy weight, the results seem to indicate there is no such thing. Even with more modern studies, such as one done by Lewis E. Hollander, Jr. on sheep, there was weight gain and then drop

---

[354]Roach, *Spook*, pg. 89-91
[355]Roach, *Spook*, pg. 93

back to the normal weight after one to six seconds.[356] At this point it seems to be a matter of flogging a dead horse, but the evidence for a material soul with weight is completely absent.

Gerry Nahum, a medical doctor and professor at Duke University, has made efforts to test for souls as well. However, he has a (somewhat) more realistic vision of being capable of testing for one. I only say realistic because he says it is necessary to attempt the procedure in a completely closed system, rather than a body upon a scale. And while Nahum has a view that testing requires more than something as simplistic as a basic scale (considering that there is weight loss associated with energy loss), it still does not help to prove that souls exist. It simply shows that, should we have a reasonable assumption to believe that souls do exist, it is difficult to be able to test for one. However, even by Nahum's assumption of a soul, which can arguably be reasoned to assume the place of "consciousness" or "mind" in his language, one bit of information, be it a thought, memory, idea, etc., would only equal "one billionth, billionth, billionth of a billionth of a kilogram.[357]

Now, a fundamental problem that arises with the concept of the soul, is that many people believe, or at least at a point did believe, that the soul was weightless, yet somehow obeyed the laws of gravity. This belief may extend as far back as to the story of *Dante's Inferno*,[358] and perhaps even before. The problem is

---

[356]Hollander, Lewis E., Jr., "Unexplained Weight Gain Transients at the Moment of Death", *Journal of Scientific Exploration*, Vol. 15, No. 4, pg. 495-500, 2001

[357]Roach, *Spook*, pg. 97-99

[358]Quinn, Gary J., *Moral Education in America: Its Future in an Age of Personal Autonomy and Multiculturalism*, iUniverse, Bloomington, IN, 2004, pg. 61

that, if something is weightless, and obeys the laws of gravity, it would not be capable of remaining in a single spot. If we look at astronauts in outer space, as an example, while they are completely material beings, they are in a constant state of free fall, as being off of a planetary body does not free them from gravity. So, if an object or being *is* weightless, then it would not be capable of remaining in a single place. But that typically is the definition of an object that is already in a state of free fall, or when there are no forces of support against our body. A person feels weight, or feels the mass of their bodies being pulled, by another object against them. This is Newton's Third Law of Motion; with every action there is an equal, but opposite, reaction. When you are walking outdoors, the sidewalk pushes back against your feet with each step. When you recline in a chair, the chair pushes back against you. Actions come in pairs.[359]

Still, if something is weightless, that is a condition of it being in a state of free fall. It is not something being without weight, but it is an object experiencing the pull of gravity with nothing to obstruct its path.[360] To be without weight, on the other hand, means it, whatever it is, would be immaterial. Even the lightest element, hydrogen, has an atomic weight of 1.007.[361] This is used to help identify how elements react and relate to other

[359]"Newton's Third Law", *Physics Classroom*, 2015, accessed May 3, 2015, http://www.physicsclassroom.com/class/newtlaws/Lesson-4/Newton-s-Third-Law
[360]"Weightlessness", *Encyclopedia Brittanica*, 2015, accessed May 3, 2015, http://www.britannica.com/EBchecked/topic/638979/weightlessness
[361]Palmer, D., "Hydrogen in the Universe", *NASA*, September 13,1997, accessed May 3, 2015, http://imagine.gsfc.nasa.gov/docs/ask_astro/answers/971113i.html

elements, but still implies the existence of some weight. I would think, based purely on conjecture, that if such a concept as that of a soul existed, it would go flying off of the face of the earth as soon as it was liberated from the weighted body, as the body would be subjected to the laws of gravity and motion. Given that Earth spins at a rate of 1000 miles (1600 kilometers) per hour,[362] it would seem an object in constant free fall would go whizzing past us.

Immaterialism is defined as something that does not consist of matter. [363] This would, typically, delve more into the philosophical side of things, but we shall explore it a bit here. The immaterial are better defined as concepts, like numbers (we can physically hold, touch, see, smell, and taste a value of something, but the number itself is something we cannot do that with), but there are still some immaterial things, hypothetically. As an example, compounds that are made up of the same chemicals, but in different orders, are called isomers. These are not immaterial things, but, should we mix around the order in which the chemicals of a substance are structured, then we are left with a different substance. As an example; C_3H_8O will, when combined in different orders, create either methoxyethane, propanol, or isopropyl (rubbing) alcohol. I think this is a poor

[362]"ASP: How Fast Are You Moving When You Are Sitting Still?", *Astronomical Society of the Pacific*, 2007, accessed May 3, 2015, http://astrosociety.org/edu/publications/tnl/71/howfast.html
[363]"Immaterial", Merriam-Webster.com, 2015, accessed May 3, 2015, http://www.merriam-webster.com/dictionary/immaterial

example of the immaterial, as there is still a material substance left in the aftermath of different combinations.[364]

On the other hand, physicist (and atheist) David Deutsch explains that something like memories are immaterial. He explains,

> *"This information can't, in my view, be reduced to statements about atoms because, if you think about what that information does, it is in brains, but the same information then gets transferred into, let's say, sound waves in air, and then it gets transferred into ink on paper, and then it gets transferred into magnetic domains inside a computer, which then control a machine that instantiates those ideas in bits of steel, and silicon, and so on. There's an immense chain of instantiations of the same information... What is being transmitted, what is having the causal effect, is not the atoms, but the fact that the atoms instantiate certain kinds of information, and not other kinds. So therefore, it is the information that is having the causal effect..."[365]*

This, I think, goes back to the issue of consciousness. It is an effect dependent on another object, and it does not mean we can then claim that outside entities are real because of thought, memory, and consciousness. Like digestion for the stomach, like sensations of touch, or memories of taste, these are all functions that are dependent on another part of the body (and uniformly from the brain). They may be immaterial, but that does not

---

[364]Heschmeyer, Joe, "Does the Immaterial Exist?", *Strange Notions*, 2012, accessed May 3, 2015, http://www.strangenotions.com/does-immaterial-exist/

[365]Hall, Amy K., "Physicist: Immaterial Explanations Aren't Necessarily False", *Stand to Reason*, October 5, 2011, http://www.str.org/blog/physicist-immaterial-explanations-aren-t-necessarily-false#.VUZ21M5N1FI

mean they are independent objects or entities that can survive the death of the body.

We have spent a great deal of time discussing the individual and his or her own soul, as well experiences through consciousness. But what of those who claim they have witnessed another person's soul, in some way, shape, or form? Well, we have perfectly rational explanations for those as well.

First, some claim to have been able to locate spirits, or ghosts, using bat detectors. [366] Bat detectors are electronic devices that depend on a bat's echolocation ultrasound signals, what a bat typically uses to detect prey or its surroundings. What becomes problematic when using one of these to detect ghosts is that there are numerous things, both alive and inanimate, that emit similar signals to bats. Inclusive of these are the obvious, bats, as well as rodents, insects, car brakes, and even TV sets.[367] To say it is possible to use bat detectors to find spirits is troubling at best — problematic and futile to be realistic.

Some people claim to have "felt a presence" in a setting believed to be haunted. Aside from the problem of "feeling" something to know that it is real; we actually know that these feelings are based on something other than a real presence of a spiritual being. In 2002, a scientist from McGill University published a study in the *Journal of Nervous and Mental Disease*. In his study, he had subjected over a thousand people to electromagnetic bursts to their right temporal lobe. When done so, the majority, roughly 80%, said they felt the presence of a

---

[366] An example of people discussing the use of bat detectors to locate "spirits":
http://alaskaghosthunting.com/index.php/forum/equipment/3-use-of-a-bat-detector-to-convert-high-freq-audio
[367] Roach, *Spook*, pg. 199

being in the room with them. Similarly, in the same year, infrared pulses were sent out into the Liverpool Metropolitan Cathedral during a concert, and people started to feel tingling on their necks, uneasy feelings in their stomachs, intense emotions, and even vision irregularities. They found that, if these pulses continued, people's eyes would vibrate and detect movement in the corners of their eyes. They found these more often in situations where the same treatment was applied, but done in older houses with thicker walls that resonate better. The same can be said of old castles, which also lack curtains and furniture that would absorb the sound frequencies. These same frequencies also have a tendency to collect, or "pool" in one area of a house, tending to make one room "feel" more haunted than the rest.[368]

A frequency known as infrasound, which is a sound below 20 hertz, can cause curtailing, or limiting, of blood to the ends of your limbs, and the limbs themselves, which is what brings on chills, unease, and even rapid heart rhythm. In high doses, this can also lead to the vibrating vision causing the individual to think they see movement when there is none, like with ultrasounds. It can also cause gagging, nausea, and salivating. And like the ultrasounds, there are natural explanations for where they come from. Church organs, elephants, whales, rhinos, and even tigers produce these low frequencies![369] So much for hauntings.

---

[368] Roach, *Spook*, pg. 219, 229-230
[369] Roach, *Spook*, pg. 230-234

Near Death Experiences

Other examples of "evidence" typically given for the afterlife are Near Death Experiences, or NDEs. It is hardly a matter of faith or religion, as people are recorded as having had them across all cultures in all walks of life. And while they are common, there is little to suggest it is anything more than the body's stressful response to trauma. As stated earlier, from Dr. Stenger's book *God and the Folly of Faith*, these experiences are rife with contrast and only share the similarity of seeing a great being in a different realm.

Part of the problem with using NDEs as evidence, is that only 20% of people who have events that bring them close to death experience them.[370] In one study, of 344 cardiac arrest patients, only 18% reported having an NDE.[371] So, with only a small group claiming to have something that resembles the NDE, as well as differences from culture to culture, it makes it difficult to believe that such a thing is based on truth, let alone on any one particular belief system.

Another part of the NDE is something called the OBE, or Out of Body Experience. This is an experience identified as a sensation of leaving one's body, floating, being able to pass through walls, and, sometimes, to be able to read others' thoughts. Attempts have been made to see if such a circumstance is true in surgical rooms in hospitals. Among the many reasons it is hard, proving it is difficult as such a small ratio of individuals experience NDEs, let alone OBEs — but there is something else. They have attempted to test and see if such an event can happen by placing cards with images or

---

[370]Stenger, *Folly of Faith*, pg. 236
[371]Roach, *Spook*, pg. 266-267

writing on them in a place that the patient will not see them. However, the staff can often become curious and will look, making it hard to determine if they had any influence in informing the patient what was on the cards prior to them offering a statement.

There was another instance in 2002 where a neurosurgeon named Olaf Blanke worked with a woman who suffered from epilepsy. Blanke had electrodes placed on the woman's brain to help regulate the seizures she was having. One of them was placed on the parietal lobe, specifically in the angular gyrus, which is responsible for regulating sensory information related to touch, vision, and balance. When Blanke and his team set off the electrode, the woman reported seeing herself "floating" out of her body, and seeing her legs becoming shorter. This, coupled with a report in 2004 from the University of Virginia, helped to confirm that OBEs are nothing more than experiences that can be replicated by stimulating a particular region of the brain.[372]

During the 1990s, a chemist from West Texas A&M, James Whinnery, was called to observe testing done on fighter pilots. The pilots were placed in a simulator that reenacted events during extreme circumstances, including high centrifugal force. During these simulations, the force decreases blood flow, and in turn deprives oxygen, to the brain. As a result, the pilots would pass out and, upon recovering, recall having tunnel vision and seeing a bright light at the end of a tunnel. This helped support a theory of British psychologist Susan Blackmore that anoxia, or depletion of oxygen to the brain, is partially responsible for

---

[372]Beauregard, Mario, "Near death, explained", Salon.com, April 21, 2012, accessed May 3, 2015, http://www.salon.com/2012/04/21/near_death_explained/

NDEs.[373] They also found that the use of goggles in the pilots' circumstances reduced, or eliminated, symptoms, as they applied pressure to the eyes and stopped the drop in blood pressure to the region, adding another explanation to NDEs, as loss of blood to the eyes is typically what causes tunnel vision.[374]

Ketamine, a dissociative anesthetic typically used for animals and also used as a recreational drug, can also stimulate an NDE. In a study done between 2003-2005 on a group of 125 individuals ranging in age from 22-61, a few with religious belief, some having experimented with the drug before, 50 reported having NDEs, some multiple times.[375] The reason it is believed that ketamine triggers NDEs is because it is thought that ketamine inhibits N-Methyl-D-aspartic acid, or NMDA, receptors in the brain, triggering the NDE. Though the drug *does* trigger the experience, it is reported that the hallucinations are often far more violent, and the user is much more aware that the experience is false, whereas those who experience the NDE, sans drugs, believe the experiences to be real.[376]

A closer example, in regards to drug or chemical use, is DMT, or Dimethyltryptamine. While there is a synthetic drug that replicates the effects, it is also a chemical produced in the pineal gland of the brain. We already know the pineal gland is responsible for some levels of NDEs, as we have already discussed, so it makes sense, then, that a chemical produced

---

[373]Ibid.

[374]Stenger, *Folly of Faith*, pg. 231

[375]Corazza, O., and Schifano, F., "Near-death states reported in a sample of 50 misusers", *Department of Clinical Pharmacology, US National Library of Medicine,* May 2010, accessed May 3, 2015, http://www.ncbi.nlm.nih.gov/pubmed/20397876

[376]Beauregard, "Near death, explained"

within the same hemisphere would trigger such a reaction. In 2000, a study by Dr. Rick Strassman on DMT was published, titled *DMT: the Spirit Molecule.* In his study, he administered approximately 400 intravenous doses of DMT to a small group of 60 volunteers, from 1990 to 1995. His observations, among many, included that DMT "exists in all of our bodies and occurs throughout the plant and animal kingdoms. It is a part of the normal makeup of humans and other mammals; marine animals; grasses and peas; toads and frogs; mushrooms and molds; and barks, flowers, and roots."[377]

When asked why the brain would naturally create DMT, and what its purpose was, Strassman said, "I think we need something in the brain that does what seems to happen to us at various times in our lives. Like silicon in computer chips, DMT is the best material for the purpose of seemingly providing access to free-standing non-corporeal realms. On the other hand, since we are all making DMT all of the time, it may also mediate our perception of everyday reality." Strassman also acknowledges that the drug is released into our systems during times of stress, and also likely during our dreams. This could be why, as our bodies go through the process of dying, or are near death, we may experience visions or feelings of euphoria — in order to relax us as our bodies, pardon the expression, give up the ghost.[378]

Despite all this knowledge and research put into what causes NDEs, people continue to tout the experiences as being legitimate and providing evidence of an afterlife. What is more

---

[377]Tao, Lin, "DMT: You Cannot Imagine a Stranger Drug or a Stranger Experience", *Vice*, August 6, 2024, accessed May 3, 2015
[378]Ibid.

troubling is the people coming from the medical field and espousing personal experiences of NDEs, arguing that they are legitimate because, as people of medicine, they would know what their bodies are actually going through. And an NDE is the most likely situation, according to them.

Take, for example, Eben Alexander, a neurosurgeon who was in a meningitis-induced coma that led to an OBE. He wrote an account of his NDE in the book titled *Proof of Heaven: A Neurosurgeon's Journey into the Afterlife.* He claims, among other things, that he saw his deceased sister, angels, and butterflies. And while it might be of value to consider the opinion of an expert in neuroscience when it comes to consciousness, and think about how he views it as independent of the brain, it is also telling to see how sloppy, unprofessional, and utterly dishonest Alexander has been in his work, outside of writing. *Esquire* magazine reported in its August 2013 edition that Alexander had been let go from several hospitals, was placed on suspension by others, and faced malpractice suits for altering records to hide medical errors, among other incidents. *Esquire* reported:

> *On August 6, 2008, the patient filed a $3 million lawsuit against Alexander, accusing him of negligence, battery, spoliation, and fraud. The purported cover-up, the changes Alexander had made to the surgical report, was a major aspect of the suit. Once again, a lawyer was accusing Alexander of altering the historical record when the historical record didn't fit the story he wanted to tell.* [379]

---

[379] Dittrich, Luke, "the Prophet: An Investigation of Eben Alexander, Author of the Blockbuster 'Proof of Heaven'", *Esquire*, Hearst Communications, Inc., New York, NY, August 2013, pg. 95

And, despite Alexander's account of losing brain activity and being clinically dead during his experience, the doctors that attended to him said he was completely conscious during the event, though he was very likely hallucinating. From the article:

> *In one chapter Dr. Alexander writes about screaming out 'God help me!' — a claim contradicted by the emergency room physician treating him that day.*
>
> *Dr. Laura Potter said she had no recollection of him crying out, plus she had intubated him — making it impossible for him to speak.*
>
> *Alexander also writes that he slipped into the coma as a result of E. coli bacterial meningitis and had no higher brain activity, while Dr. Potter says the coma was medically induced and the patient was conscious, though hallucinating.*[380]

Sam Harris, the well-known atheist, neuroscientist, and philosopher (being one of the "four horsemen" of the New Atheism movement), took Alexander's claims and made the following statement:

> *"Everything—absolutely everything—in Alexander's account rests on repeated assertions that his visions of heaven occurred while his cerebral cortex was "shut down," "inactivated," "completely shut down," "totally offline," and "stunned to complete inactivity." The evidence he provides for this claim is not only inadequate—it suggests that he doesn't know anything about the relevant brain science...Coma is not associated with the complete cessation of cortical activity, in any case. And to my knowledge, almost no one*

---

[380]"Was 'Proof of Heaven' author hallucinating?", *Daily Mail*, July 2, 2013, accessed May 5, 2015, http://www.dailymail.co.uk/news/article-2354351/Proof-Heaven-author-multiple-claims-book-debunked-doctor-treated-seven-day-coma.html

thinks that consciousness is purely a matter of cortical activity...Even if his entire cortex had truly shut down (again, an incredible claim), how can he know that his visions didn't occur in the minutes and hours during which its functions returned?[381]

And, for those who think Harris to be a bit too militant in his views, a neurologist by the name of Oliver Sacks agreed with Harris. In his article "Seeing God in the Third Millennium" for *the Atlantic.*

...a hallucinatory journey to the bright light and beyond, a full-blown NDE, can occur in 20 or 30 seconds, even though it seems to last much longer. Subjectively, during such a crisis, the very concept of time may seem variable or meaningless. The one most plausible hypothesis in Dr. Alexander's case, then, is that his NDE occurred not during his coma, but as he was surfacing from the coma and his cortex was returning to full function. It is curious that he does not allow this obvious and natural explanation, but instead insists on a supernatural one.[382]

Sacks' article also offers some great insight into how the mind creates experiences found in NDE claims. He includes quotes, one from Fyodor Dostoevsky, about epileptic seizures that bring on such experiences.

The air was filled with a big noise and I tried to move. I felt the heaven was going down upon the earth and that it engulfed me. I have really touched God.

[381]Harris, Sam, "This Must Be Heaven", SamHarris.org, October 12, 2012, accessed May 5, 2015, http://www.samharris.org/blog/item/this-must-be-heaven

[382]Sacks, Oliver, "Seeing God in the Third Millenium", *the Atlantic*, December 12, 2012, accessed May 5, 2015, http://www.theatlantic.com/health/archive/2012/12/seeing-god-in-the-third-millennium/266134/

> *He came into me myself, yes God exists, I cried, and I don't remember anything else. You all, healthy people ... can't imagine the happiness which we epileptics feel during the second before our fit. ... I don't know if this felicity lasts for seconds, hours or months, but believe me, for all the joys that life may bring, I would not exchange this one.*

Though Sacks speaks about how incredible this phenomenon is, he also notes that it is extremely rare — more so than the results of people who experience NDEs in the larger studies, averaging one to two percent in patients with temporal lobe epilepsy. And, as noted with Alexander's claim, Sacks says that NDEs and OBEs are known to occur during the "waking" periods of consciousness, in which the patient's mental state is severely altered. He also points out that these hallucinations activate the same points in the brain that normal perceptions do. This may be why, as discussed before, they are taken to be more real than when recreational drugs are used to stimulate similar experiences.[383]

Another test done on rats showed that, just before dying, the subjects suddenly had a burst of brain activity. Researchers planted electrodes within the rats' brains and administered lethal injections. Just after the rats' hearts stopped, their brains lit up with activity, extending their consciousness into a type of "hyperconsciousness." While it does not demonstrate that the rats experienced any sort of euphoric sensation, or visions of seeing another world, by the researchers' own admission it does

---

[383]Ibid.

provide some possible insight into what may be happening in a human mind right as the body starts to die.[384]

Something to consider, as well, is that not all NDEs are positive experiences. Of all the reports of NDEs, 23% describe unpleasant experiences. These are subject to the same shortcomings as other experiences, but we also run into the problem of them being reported far less than positive experiences. People will often not report them because it creates anxiety, and this also does not take into account that they are given far less consideration and attention than the positive ones. They also make data collecting difficult, as most are not reported until years after the experience. Though self-reported instances are not the most reliable, making the case by being dependent on the individual's memory proves another challenge, as memory is the least reliable evidence in scientific study.[385]

We also must take into consideration things like how a mafia hitman experienced a pleasant NDE. He had been shot in the chest and was left to die, but had a positive NDE where he "felt the presence of God and unconditional love." After this experience, he stopped working for the mob and took up counseling.[386] So we need to consider, now, why would this individual experience the presence of God and feelings of love if

---

[384]Stein, Rob, "Brains of Dying Rats Yield Clues About Near-Death Experiences", NPR.org, August 12, 2013, accessed May 5, 2015, http://www.npr.org/blogs/health/2013/08/12/211324316/brains-of-dying-rats-yield-clues-about-near-death-experiences

[385]Lichfield, Gideon, "the Science of Near-Death Experiences: Empirically investigating brushes with the afterlife", the Atlantic, April 2015, accessed May 5, 2015, http://www.theatlantic.com/features/archive/2015/03/the-science-of-near-death-experiences/386231/

[386]Roach, Spook, pg. 288

he were doing things as immoral as murder? By our own standards, and assuming that the afterlife exists, would we not expect this person to see hell? Would we not expect him to be tortured and tormented?

We are delving a bit into the philosophical side, but it is necessary in order to understand what this can mean. First, it could mean that, assuming an afterlife exists, this man was not as bad as we think him to be. He could have been murdering people who abuse children, puppies, and spouses. Perhaps he was eliminating potential terrorist threats — people who were targeting government buildings and public servants, hospitals, or even schools.

Second, maybe God, assuming there is one, wanted him to experience the afterlife in order to turn his life around, as that is what he ended up doing. God, perhaps, knew he was capable of doing good, but simply needed to give him the motivation he needed, similar to how I offer my daughter treats in order to get her to behave appropriately.

A third possibility could be that, assuming there is a God, he made a mistake. Maybe he misdirected the mobster's soul into heaven amid a flurry of other actions we can be sure he was performing. I mean, if he can overlook impoverished children in Africa in favor of helping a sports team achieve victory in the Super Bowl, then it seems likely he might accidentally welcome a villain into the heavenly realm. I mean, this *is* the same God that left Adam and Eve unattended in the Garden of Eden with a talking serpent to tempt them into eating from the one tree from which they were forbidden to eat. Mistakes happen, so we can overlook God accidentally giving a murderer a peek into paradise.

A fourth possibility is that, after looking at the science behind NDEs, we know what this mobster experienced was purely a psychological process due to stress, low oxygen, and, very likely, low blood pressure to the brain and eyes. We can assume his body, and consciousness, were going through the natural stages they would typically go through if they were in the process of dying, or at least starting to die. Personally, I am of the opinion, given what we can and do know about our bodies and the capabilities of our consciousness at such a point, that this is the most likely of scenarios.

Quantum Field Theory

Quantum Field Theory (QFT) is, according to the *Encyclopedia Britannica* definition, a "body of physical principles combining the elements of quantum mechanics with those of relativity to explain the behavior of subatomic particles and their interactions via a variety of force fields."[387] There is a lot to unpack from this statement, even in such a short definition. So, let us start with an idea of what the elements of this study are.

Quantum mechanics is a study of physics aimed at the very small. And we are not talking about teacup Chihuahuas, adorable as they may be (on a purely subjective level); instead, we are talking about studying how the natural world works on an atomic, and even subatomic, level. Prior to the understanding, or focus, of this field, there was a scientist by the name of Max Planck who, despite what he knew about physics, could not understand why a closed box, when heated in a proper way, would not produce an infinite amount of ultraviolet

---

[387]"quantum field theory", *Encyclopedia Britannica Online*, 2015, accessed May 5, 2015,
http://www.britannica.com/EBchecked/topic/486221/quantum-field-theory

radiation. Though it may have radiated various colors, there was no infinite amount of ultraviolet radiation, or anything else. In an act of what he described as "desperation," Planck changed the math in his equation to demonstrate that there was a finite, or "quanta," amount of energy. With this consideration in place, the equation, and experiment, worked. Albert Einstein even jumped on board (though he struggled to be able to fully grasp the study), and said there must be individual particles, rather than just waves, of things like energy and light. These particles were labelled "photons" by Berkeley physicist Gilbert Lewis in 1926.[388]

Quantum mechanics has an interesting interpretation of how things, like photons or electrons, function. Though they work as both a particle and/or a wave, they are truly neither. Or at least they are neither, until we look at them and can view them as being either a particle or wave. There is a famous thought experiment done by physicist Erwin Schrödinger involving a cat, a box, and poison, among a few other items, that accurately demonstrates this idea. It goes as follows: a cat is placed into a box with a Geiger counter, an instrument that detects radiation. Also placed in the box is a vial of poison, a hammer, and a radioactive substance. After radioactive decay happens in the box, the Geiger counter detects it, activates the hammer which releases the poison, and subsequently kills the cat. It sounds simple enough, but the decay process of radioactive elements is random with no way to predict the timeline when it would happen. So it exists in a state of "superposition," meaning it is "decayed" and "not decayed" at

---

[388]"Quantum Mechanics", *the American Institute of Physics*, via PBS, 1999, accessed May 5, 2015, http://www.pbs.org/transistor/science/info/quantum.html

the same time. The question becomes, is the cat dead or not after you start the process? We have no way of telling unless we look inside the box to see the cat. The cat becomes in as much a state of superposition as the radioactive elements and, as such, the cat is both alive and dead at the same time since we cannot predict when the decay will happen.[389]

Part of the quantum mechanics field, and the first step into quantum field theory, is quantum electrodynamics. Quantum electrodynamics describes, mathematically, how light interacts with matter and how charged particles interact with one another. What is needed to consider this aspect of quantum mechanics is the knowledge that it is all relativistic, meaning Einstein's theory of special relativity is built into the equations for QED.[390] Special relativity is limited to objects in inertial movement, or moving in a straight line at a constant speed.[391] A lot of the experiments with QED involve a particle known as a muon, one similar to the electron but 207 times heavier. The muon has an incredibly short life, 2.2 microseconds, before it decays into an electron and two different types of neutrinos and performs the

---

[389]Kramer, Melody, "the Physics Behind Schrödinger's Cat Paradox", *National Geographic*, August 14, 2013, accessed May 5, 2015, http://news.nationalgeographic.com/news/2013/08/130812-physics-schrodinger-erwin-google-doodle-cat-paradox-science/

[390]"Quantum electrodynamics", *Encyclopedia Brittanica Online*, 2015, accessed May 5, 2015, http://www.britannica.com/EBchecked/topic/486203/quantum-electrodynamics-QED

[391]"Special relativity", *Encyclopedia Brittanica Online*, 2015, accessed May 5, 2015, http://www.britannica.com/EBchecked/topic/558565/special-relativity

process of ionization in atoms.[392] QED relies on the fact that charged particles both give off and absorb photons, which transmit electromagnetic force. Photons may be released, either as light or another form of electromagnetic radiation, which is why Einstein's special relativity is put into the equation. And, if I may quote *Encyclopedia Britannica*, "The magnetic moment of this type of particle has been shown to agree with the theory to nine significant digits. Agreement of such high accuracy makes QED one of the most successful physical theories so far devised."[393] This is important to note, as it helps us understand how well we know the theory and how it helps us know, even with a field as new and with so much still to learn as quantum mechanics, this is an area we can demonstrate as being reliable and something to help us in understanding why it makes the afterlife seem improbable, if not a false theory or belief.

Now there are two sides to quantum field theory, to help narrow this down a bit. There is the "ordinary, non-relativistic quantum theory," which specializes in the side of quantum mechanics that Schrödinger's cat comes from. On the other end of the spectrum, which makes up the majority of field theorists, are the two groups split into either "intuitive" (or "axiomatic") or "heuristic" areas of QFT.[394] Axiomatic QFT seeks to make everything in the study mathematically precise, but has its shortcomings as the field of quantum mechanics has proven to

[392]"muon", *Encyclopedia Brittanica Online*, 2015, accessed May 5, 2015, http://www.britannica.com/EBchecked/topic/397734/muon
[393]"Quantum electrodynamics", 2015
[394]Norton, John D., "Quantum field theory workshop", *Center for Philosophy of Science*, October 14-15, 2011, accessed May 5, 2015, http://www.pitt.edu/~pittcntr/Being_here/last_donut/donut_2011-12/10-14-11_qft.html

be, often, fairly unpredictable. Heuristic QFT is the more populated area of study by quantum physicists — an area that attempts to match predictions to the observable data.[395] In other words, one field, the one less focused on absolute precision, gets the most results; hence why more quantum physicists are focused on that area of study.

Now, to look specifically at what QFT is, we need to know a certain thing about the different particles, or waves, as understood by quantum mechanics. First, when we talk about "waves" and "particles," we speak about them, as stated before with photons, as a sort of unknown unless we look directly at them. They function as either, but they are more like a short vibration within the field. So, in the photon field, a photon is not a particle, nor is it really, truly a wave, but a short vibration within that field. We see a similar thing with all types of particles in various fields: a muon field, electron field, quark field, and so on. And this is something that is known to cover the entire universe. In other words, this is not something we merely find in a small, localized setting under specific conditions; we can go anywhere, investigate a particular field (quark, photon, etc.), and find it wherever that is.[396]

Think of it this way, and I shall use the example given in PBS' "the Good Vibrations of Quantum Field Theories" (2013,

[395]Carroll, Sean, "How To Think About Quantum Field Theory", *Discover: Science for the Curious,* February 7, 2013, accessed May 5, 2015,
http://blogs.discovermagazine.com/cosmicvariance/2012/02/07/how-to-think-about-quantum-field-theory/#.VUkC4Y5VgSU
[396]Lincoln, Don, "the Good Vibrations of Quantum Field Theories", *PBS*, August 5, 2013, accessed May 5, 2015,
http://www.pbs.org/wgbh/nova/blogs/physics/2013/08/the-good-vibrations-of-quantum-field-theories/

PBS.org). Imagine, if you will, two men standing in two different boats in a lake. One of them has a sack of potatoes and throws it to the other. When this action occurs, the boat that the man who originally had the potatoes was in creates ripples and waves, which then affect the other boat, and the person in the boat catching it. So, in our example of the photon vibrating, when it does so, it affects the other surrounding photons, both in vibrations and momentum. Photons are also capable of affecting other particles in different fields, namely charged particles, but not gluons or neutrinos. The photon, however, *can* disrupt the gluon field, but only by creating a quark vibration that, in turn, may make a gluon vibration[397] — a sort of particle version of a telephone, if you will.

This is all fascinating, incredible stuff to understand. But, you may be wondering, what does this have to do with our study of the afterlife? Well, it has a lot to do with it. First, because there is nothing in the laws of physics that would permit for any of the information we carry in our consciousness to continue on in any way, shape, or form, after we die. If we did have a soul, or something of that nature that did carry our mind or consciousness, we would be able to detect it through the QFT. We are able to detect photons, things that appear in the physical world out of nothingness (if only for a few microseconds), and we are able to see other particles that are on such a microscopic scale, so we should be able to detect the vibrations, the fields, the particles of the soul. Even if it were not immediately detectable, it would be possible to find it through the vibrations and interactions of particles with other particles and fields, especially since people hold so tightly to the view that the soul,

---

[397]Ibid.

though being immaterial, affects something material — namely our brain/mind and physical body. So, if we are to assume that a soul is real, we then need to be able to answer not only what particles, vibrations, or bits the soul is made up of, but also how that interacts with other matter in the universe and what holds it together.[398]

According to the Dirac equation, the equation that describes a subset of fermions (the particles that make up matter), parity (the opposite of a spatial coordinate in three dimensions) is symmetrical and the equation, in and of itself, is demonstrably true in quantum mechanics and special relativity (both necessary for QFT).[399] Every experiment done in quantum mechanics, involving electrons, everyday high energies, and this equation, has proven to be correct. In order for souls to exist, for the concept to be one that can be worked out, the believer needs to prove that the Dirac equation is incorrect. Given that the equation has been proven correct, again, in every experiment done for the sake of quantum mechanics and special relativity with relation to electrons in everyday energies, it seems highly unlikely such a thing can be done.[400]

Sean Carroll, a research professor at the California Institute of Technology, asks some great questions about the soul that should be, but never are, taken into consideration when people proclaim that the soul is real. First, does the soul have a

---

[398]Carroll, Sean, "Physics and the Immortality of the Soul", *Scientific American*, May 23, 2011, accessed May 6, 2015, http://blogs.scientificamerican.com/guest-blog/2011/05/23/physics-and-the-immortality-of-the-soul/

[399]Atkins, P.W., *Quanta: A Handbook of Concepts,* Oxford University Press, New York, NY, 1974, pg. 52

[400]Carroll, "Physics and the Immortality of the Soul", 2011

Hamiltonian? A Hamiltonian is an operator that corresponds with the total energy of a system; the sum of the kinetic energy of all particles in a system, plus the potential energy. Does a soul's interactions with unitarity, that which prevents allowed evolution of systems to ensure that the sum probabilities of an outcome of an event is one, preserve the conservation of information? How do the neurons in our minds, carrying our thoughts and consciousness, attach on to something that is immaterial?[401]

Breaking away from quantum mechanics for a moment, and into evolutionary biology, we are faced with other scientific questions. Theologians, as we discussed earlier in our study, have postulated that we do not have a soul, or that we don't reach ensoulment, until a certain point in utero. Whether it is at conception, or at forty days, seems beside the point. But we can see that it is not believed that the sperm or egg, prior to our conception, come equipped with souls. Did our ancestors have souls? I do not mean our ancestors that lived centuries before us, but the ancestors of humanity. Did Homo erectus have a soul? Homo habilis? Australopithecus afarensis?[402] Did any members of the great ape family before us have souls? What about the lizard and bird families? Aquatic life? Amoebas? Single-celled organisms? Where along these lines did souls come in to play? If it is believed we are the only species to have, or have had, them, then we need to start rethinking the concept of the soul in life.

---

[401]Ibid.

[402]McAfee, David G.,
https://www.facebook.com/AuthorDavidGMcAfee/photos/a.46392936
0306066.107855.207237099308628/455939567771712 , posted
September 3, 2012, accessed September 11, 2015

What we truly need to realize, on the quantum, biological, physical, and very real level, is that humanity is no different than any other animal that ever was or ever will be. We are not the exception to the rule; we are very much a part of the rule. The laws of physics and quantum mechanics dictate that there is no room for the possibility for a soul — a life beyond life. If there were, we would have been able to detect that which makes up the soul and how it functions with the matter of all else there is in the universe. We know because, among other reasons, the mind is part, or a function, of the brain (maybe it even *is* the brain). The brain is made up of atoms, as are all other "things" (for a lack of a better term) in this world, and when we die, there is no way for us to continue on. We know this because we know how the atoms in our bodies work. And since there is no evidence to show that the atoms in our mind are taken on by an immaterial, or material, thing, we know that there is no such thing as an afterlife. The science is clear, and we know that there are no new particles, no new fields, quarks, life systems, or anything that would interfere with our minds or affect our lives; and that is because we know all the relevant information about the atoms in our minds, in our bodies, and in the material world around us. If anything new *were* to be introduced, it would not have a profound enough effect, or any effect, that would alter what we do know about the mind and life after death.[403]

Sean Carroll, who I realize I have been referencing to quite some extent from various posts up to this point, provides the excellent closure that this part of the discussion deserves.

---

[403]"Sean Carroll On Death And The Afterlife" from Zehadi Alam, March 14, 2015, accessed May 6, 2015,
https://www.youtube.com/watch?v=uQNnvfMJd_Y

"Nobody ever asks these questions out loud, possibly because of how silly they sound. Once you start asking them, the choice you are faced with becomes clear: either overthrow everything we think we have learned about modern physics, or distrust the stew of religious accounts/unreliable testimony/wishful thinking that makes people believe in the possibility of life after death. It's not a difficult decision, as scientific theory-choice goes...There's no reason to be agnostic about ideas that are dramatically incompatible with everything we know about modern science. Once we get over any reluctance to face reality on this issue, we can get down to the much more interesting questions of how human beings and consciousness really work."[404]

What Science Says Happens When We Die

I will gladly be the first to admit that none of this is very reassuring and is, in fact, a rather bleak outlook on what follows once we stop being alive. As a conscious human being, who really only had a small taste of what it was like to not exist, I will say that it is worrisome to think, to know, that one day I will no longer be able to feel, sense, observe, or, in general, just be conscious of the world and myself. But that does not mean there isn't a sense of peace, calm, and restfulness I can gain by understanding, and even accepting, what will happen to me after I die.

What we must understand, and this is taking a philosophical stance first, is that we cannot imagine a life that would be worth living for an eternity. What I mean is, even in such a short time of just a few years, I, myself, have changed what matters most to me and what I enjoy. While I was in my twenties, I was very

---

[404]Carroll, "Physics and the Immortality of the Soul", 2011

much into music; I studied it in college, I learned numerous instruments and performance techniques, I recorded music and toured the country, I even became a music teacher. However, today, in my thirties, I enjoy a quiet life of reading, researching, and putting together books or short writings that explore issues related to theology and human rights. Perhaps it is because I went from a rather hedonistic "what matters is the experience I get out of this" to an "oops, my actions have consequences" mentality.

Also, considering how much I used to move around on stage; throwing my guitar, leaping off of things, flipping over my band-mates, that is simply not something I am capable of doing anymore, given how my body reacts to physical exertion. Not only because of my heart condition (though I must admit I am surprised at what I was capable of doing then, given my limitations), but now that my joints do not allow for as much movement, let alone what I am capable of doing muscle wise. It is a matter of fact we all face; as we get older, our bodies start to weaken and deteriorate. I may develop arthritis later in life, keeping me from being able to play several of the instruments I enjoy playing. I might develop Alzheimer's and not have the mental capacity to remember how to play, or other things I enjoy doing now in my life. Perhaps my diabetes worsens to a point where I end up needing limbs removed (hopefully I will remain wise enough to manage my treatment and diet to avoid such a thing), or maybe my heart condition worsens to a point where I am incapable of doing much beyond walking. A lot of ifs, but all, certainly, not out of the realm of possibility.

Now, if we assumed I did not die, but maintained the same level of progressing in weakness, I feel I would eventually be bound to a wheelchair, or perhaps a hospital bed, in permanent hospice care. Most assuredly, my mind would weaken, along with my body, to a point at which I may end up in a natural vegetative state. Even if I remained in peak physical condition, there would be a point, perhaps after a few thousand years (if I pace myself), where I would not be interested in continuing on. I would become bored, after learning all I possibly could of the world and trying everything that I was willing to or capable of trying. But I must not forget that every single person in my life, friend, foe, and family, would perish at some point. Would I be happy, comfortable even, to say goodbye and try to forget the person to be able to move on and find someone new to take their spot? Can loved ones, and those who challenge us, be replaceable like a TV set, or vehicle? My wife tells me the answer is no, so I am inclined to say as much. I have had a difficult enough time dealing with the loss of pets; forget dealing with the loss of a human I have bonded with on a much more intimate level. So, in a scenario in which we are immortal, life would become a hindrance — a burden. With this in mind, death is a good thing, indeed.

Next we have to consider the fact that, if nobody died (forget just ourselves), it would cause enormous problems. Yes, it would completely eradicate the problem of worrying about what comes after we die, but then it would entail a whole new world of problems we are not prepared to take on. First is the population issue: if humans did not die, but continued to reproduce at the average we do today (ignoring families like the Duggars, we will use the 3.13 children per household average of 2014),[405] we would have nowhere to live. Forget the 7.2 billion

---

[405]"Average size of a family in the United States from 1960 to 2014", *Statista: the Statistics Portal*, 2015, accessed May 6, 2015, http://www.statista.com/statistics/183657/average-size-of-a-family-in-the-us/

(and growing) population present in the world today. [406] Inclusive of today's population, there have been 108 billion people, roughly, to have ever walked the earth.[407] According to Harvard University's sociobiologist Edward O. Wilson, the earth could, potentially, hold only nine to ten billion based on our resources and what earth is capable of producing for food.[408] So, if no one died, either we would have depleted the earth of resources several millennia ago, or someone would have kick started our space program sooner. All hypothetical, and, obviously, the second would have been unlikely since we did not develop the ability to explore space until the last century. However, things would have been bleak under those circumstances.

I should clarify my position on this. I am not stating that we should be thrilled to die. In fact, I am quite happy to live and would be content to have a long life, but, given how my body, or really anyone's body, weakens and deteriorates over time, death would be a necessary good. And given what we have just explored with how much human life the planet can sustain, it is a necessary good for us all. That is not to say we should be

---

[406]Schlesinger, Robert, "The 2015 U.S. and World Populations", *U.S. News*, December 31, 2014, accessed May 6, 2015, http://www.usnews.com/opinion/blogs/robert-schlesinger/2014/12/31/us-population-2015-320-million-and-world-population-72-billion

[407]Johnson, George, "How Many People Ever Lived?", *Discover: Science for the Curious*, August 11, 2013, accessed May 6, 2015, http://blogs.discovermagazine.com/fire-in-the-mind/2013/08/11/how-many-people-ever-lived/#.VUpp-Y5VgSU

[408]Wolchover, Natalie, "How Many People Can Earth Support?", *Live Science,* October 11, 2011, accessed May 6, 2015, http://www.livescience.com/16493-people-planet-earth-support.html

killing ourselves, or each other, to obtain such a good. Think of it this way; if you enjoy a hamburger, or maybe ice cream or a sweet, every now and again, there is no harm in that. With a balanced diet, it is completely reasonable for you to turn to a treat every now and again. However, if you have a hamburger night after night or meal after meal, for as long as you choose, your health will deteriorate faster and will make you susceptible to developing diabetes or cancer, among other risks. It is shown that high red meat consumption does shorten one's life span. And studies have determined that, even in controlled groups, with an increase in red meat, the mortality rate jumps.[409] Studies of a diet that is heavy in sugar also shows high risk for people to die from heart disease. [410] My point is this: good things, in moderation, are good for us, but too much proves to be problematic. I would like to live a long, happy, healthy life. But should I reach a point where I am not happy, and not healthy (and the two are not mutually exclusive), death would be a good thing for me.

This stands true for us all. We are all susceptible to deteriorating health, aging, and eventually death. It is not wrong for us to want to live, but this comes back to our question posed in the section of the afterlife discussion. If we are to live, in a highly incapacitated state, and constantly ill or in pain, we then need to question if that is an acceptable way for us to do so.

[409]Wein, Harrison, "Risk in Red Meat?", *National Institute of Health*, March 26, 2012, accessed May 7, 2015,

http://www.nih.gov/researchmatters/march2012/03262012meat.htm

[410]Corliss, Julie, "Eating too much added sugar increases the risk of dying with heart disease", *Harvard Health Publications*, February 6, 2014, accessed May 7, 2015,

http://www.health.harvard.edu/blog/eating-too-much-added-sugar-increases-the-risk-of-dying-with-heart-disease-201402067021

With the philosophical issue out of the way, we now need to turn to the rather gory side of death and what happens to our physical bodies after we die. It is fascinating, but certainly not the most pleasant discussion. So, I warn you, prepare for some bad news before we get to the good.

When we die, we go through a few stages. The first is called "clinical death," and is the type of stage that I, myself, went through with my own incident. This stage is during the first four to six minutes, and is one that a body, if it is capable of doing so, can survive. I am an obvious example of this. This stage is characterized by the lungs no longer taking in air and the heart no longer beating. Even though these things happen, there is often enough oxygen still in the brain to prevent damage from occurring, as well as keep parts like the eyes and kidneys alive for a few extra minutes.[411] During this time, the brain also goes through a final surge of activity, using up what oxygen remains. This is what we saw with the experiment with the rats, and it may explain, for those that do survive this first stage, why there are certain experiences and visions. And though the oxygen is depleted in the brain, the hormones that control body function also stop being sent out, and some body movement and functions may still happen for the first few minutes after death.[412]

Following clinical death is the second stage: biological death. This is the point where, due to oxygen no longer being brought

---

[411]Palermo, Elizabeth, "What Happens When You Die?", *Live Science,* January 29, 2014, accessed May 6, 2015,
http://www.livescience.com/42955-what-happens-when-you-die.html
[412]"What Happens When You Die?", *Discovery News*, October 30, 2014, accessed May 6, 2015,
https://www.youtube.com/watch?v=nqOITqLfnkc

in, and the heart no longer circulating the blood to bring oxygen to any part of the body, cells start to degenerate and the body's organs shut down.[413] It is this point when the muscles in the body relax, as there is no oxygen coming in for them to burn for tension. Among these muscles are the sphincter and detrusor muscles in the bladder. And, as I am sure you have guessed, this results in the deceased voiding these parts of their body upon death.[414]

Even though our bodies may be dead, there are still living bacteria, both on our skin, and in our digestive tract. For every cell we have in our body, there are roughly ten living, single-celled microbes crawling around in our digestive tract alone.[415] There are, roughly, 37.2 *trillion* cells in the human body.[416] So that means we have almost half a quadrillion microbes alive in our digestive tract when we die, left alone to eat away at our flesh. But that is only in our digestive tract; we also have skin bacteria that are alive and left to feast on us after we pass. And the bacteria change from area to area; while we will see more on the wetter, or more damp, parts of our body, like under the arms or in the belly button, we still find other kinds in the folds of our skin, on our eyebrows, and even in our nose. Our nose, it should be pointed out, would be like the rainforest of our bodies; teeming with diversified microorganisms that will, eventually,

[413]Palermo, "What Happens...", 2014
[414]"What Happens...", *Discovery News,* 2014
[415]Ibid.
[416]Eveleth, Rose, "There are 37.2 Trillion Cells in Your Body", Smithsonian.com, October 24, 2013, accessed May 7, 2015, http://www.smithsonianmag.com/smart-news/there-are-372-trillion-cells-in-your-body-4941473/?no-ist

start eating away at your flesh upon expiration.[417] If you think this is gross, just wait.

What follows, within the first hour after death, is something called the "death chill," or algor mortis. The human body should, naturally, have a temperature of 98.6 degrees Fahrenheit, or 37 degrees Celsius. After death, with no heart beat to circulate the blood and oxygen, the body starts to cool at roughly 1.5 degrees Fahrenheit, or .83 degrees Celsius per hour, until it reaches room temperature.[418] That is only the average; if the person is thin or malnourished, or if the climate they die in is cold, the process is sped up. Likewise, if the person was obese, or was in warmer, or more humid, climates, the process is slowed.[419]

After that, the body starts the lividity process. Again, due to the heart beat stopping, all the fluids in the body stop moving and in turn start to accumulate at the lowest point in the body. As a result, the skin in the area where the blood gathers turns purple. This all happens within thirty minutes to two hours after death.[420] This blood also starts to clot, which is what helps forensic experts tell if a body has been moved since the person died.[421]

---

[417]Harris, Richard, "World of Bacteria, Alive on Your Skin", NPR.org, May 28, 2009, accessed May 7, 2015, http://www.npr.org/templates/story/story.php?storyId=104662183

[418]"What Happens...", *Discovery News*, 2014

[419]"algor mortis", *the American Heritage Medical Dictionary*, 2007, accessed May 7, 2015, http://medical-dictionary.thefreedictionary.com/algor+mortis

[420]"postmortem lividity", *Mosby's Medical Dictionary, Eighth Edition*, 2009, accessed May 7, 2015, http://medical-dictionary.thefreedictionary.com/postmortem+lividity

[421]"What Happens...", *Discovery News*, 2014

In hours three and four, rigor mortis, also called postmortem rigidity, sets in. This is the muscles, and skeletal system, stiffening after death. This happens because, after death, calcium, specifically myosinogen and paramyosinogen, rushes and coagulates into the tissue of the muscles, bonding with proteins that control the contraction of muscles. [422] This, typically, lasts for 24-48 hours after it sets in, but can last up to a week, depending on when decomposition starts. The eyes will also start to cloud, especially if left open. Though studies have determined that roughly 63% of people close their eyes completely after dying.[423]

During this time, our skin cells start to die away, in a process known as "necrosis," thanks to a lack of blood circulation, resulting in in body's inability to clean up the dead cells as it typically would if blood was flowing normally. This can happen while a person is alive too, if blood is not flowing properly to a specific part of the body. In either case, what ends up resulting is the death of skin, and eventually of body parts and limbs themselves, which is also known as gangrene.[424] If you are alive, gangrene is something a person would really want looked at. If not for the fact that they are losing a limb or body part, then because it could be caused by a recent surgery gone awry, diabetes, a blood vessel disease, suppressed immune system, or even a serious injury. If that is not bad enough, not having it

---

[422]"postmortem rigidity", *the American Heritage Medical Dictionary*, 2007, accessed May 7, 2015, http://medical-dictionary.thefreedictionary.com/postmortem+rigidity

[423]"What Happens...", *Discovery News, 2014*

[424]Vorvick, Linda J., MD, "Necrosis", *Medline Plus: the U.S. National Library of Medicine*, August 11, 2013, accessed May 7, 2015, http://www.nlm.nih.gov/medlineplus/ency/article/002266.htm

treated could cause the gangrene to spread or even result in the person's death.[425] At that point, gangrene would be happening naturally anyway.

Cell death is not just happening on the surface; inside our bodies, carbon dioxide levels rise along with the pH levels. This weakens the cells to the point of having their membranes rupture, forcing blister-like fluids, rich in nutrients, into the surrounding tissue.[426] Blisters, tissue damage, and color change are a result of this happening. Eventually, not necessarily during this same time, because of the process of necrosis, the skin color will go from green, to purple, and eventually to black.[427]

We are only, now, about two or three days in to the process of bodily decay after death. Amazing, right? But at this stage, we are faced with a process known as "putrefaction." Putrefaction comes from the Latin *puter*, meaning "rotten," and *facere*, meaning "to make." It is called this because, as there is a lack of oxygen within the body, having been depleted by the organisms living in various sections of the body at the time of death, they start to spread out in order to find more nourishment, and to locate more oxygen-rich blood. This results in some of them decaying and producing awful-smelling gasses and compounds. Among these are ammonia, sulfur, freon, and hydrogen sulfide.[428] [429] To make this an even less pleasant-smelling

[425]Yvas, Jatin M., MD, "Gangrene", *Medline Plus: the U.S. National Library of Medicine*, September 1, 2013, accessed May 7, 2015, http://www.nlm.nih.gov/medlineplus/ency/article/007218.htm

[426]Fischetti, Mark, "What Happens to Your Body after You Die?", *Scientific American*, April 7, 2014, accessed May 6, 2015, http://www.scientificamerican.com/video/what-happens-to-your-body-after-you-die/

[427]"What Happens...", *Discovery News, 2014*

[428]Fischetti, *Scientific American*, 2014

experience, there is a sort of zombie-like process where, in areas like the pancreas and stomach, the enzymes and bacteria that the organs create eat them. And the consequence of that is the abdomen turns green, gasses build up, and non-edible, or non-digestible, elements are forced out of the various orifices of the body. This would include any excrement, or undigested food, being sent out of the body.[430]

During this process, there are two organic chemicals that are produced in the body. One is putrescine: a colorless, foul-smelling, toxic gas typically found in decaying tissue and fecal matter, as a result of the decomposition of ornithine,[431] an important amino acid needed for the formation of urea,[432] a byproduct of protein metabolism.[433] The other gas is cadaverine, a nontoxic, syrupy substance known to come from decaying flesh as a result of the bacterial process.[434] These chemicals end up working their way into the blood stream, making it into many

---

[429]"Putrefaction", *the American Heritage Medical Dictionary*, 2007, accessed May 7, 2015, http://medical-dictionary.thefreedictionary.com/Putrefaction

[430]"What Happens...", *Discovery News,* 2014

[431]"Putrescine", *Mosby's Medical Dictionary, Eighth Edition*, 2009, accessed May 7, 2015, http://medical-dictionary.thefreedictionary.com/putrescine

[432]"Ornithine", *the American Heritage Medical Dictionary*, 2007, accessed May 7, 2015, http://medical-dictionary.thefreedictionary.com/ornithine

[433]"Urea", *the American Heritage Medical Dictionary*, 2007, accessed May 7, 2015, http://medical-dictionary.thefreedictionary.com/urea

[434]"Cadaverine", *the American Heritage Medical Dictionary*, 2007, accessed May 7, 2015, http://medical-dictionary.thefreedictionary.com/cadaverine

parts of the body, and oozing out any open holes in the flesh or orifices.[435]

This is incredibly disgusting, and the smell is equally foul. But, because of the smell, more insects, like blow flies and beetles, come and lay eggs within the corpse. To an extent, this is likely already happening, but now being done in larger quantities. Think of it like an insects exodus to the promised land of gross, decaying flesh. What happens now is that the insects lay their eggs within the rotting flesh; some will lay several hundred that all will hatch within a day. The larvae, once hatched as maggots, will eat the surrounding flesh for up to a week before becoming a grown insect and leaving the corpse. The result includes approximately 60% of the body's flesh being eaten, and more opportunities for gasses and smells to be released.[436]

After all this starts a process, much like a natural mummification, called butyric fermentation. During this process, the organs that are left dry and wax over. This turns the carbohydrates left over in the flesh into butyric acid.[437] The smell resembles rancid butter or parmesan cheese,[438] and it proves to be a rather enticing smell to enzymes, as they slowly start to digest the remaining organs. This process can take up to a year in normal climates, but will increase, or decrease,

---

[435]"What Happens...", *Discovery News*, 2014

[436]Ibid.

[437]"Butyric fermentation", *Mosby's Medical Dictionary, Eighth Edition*, 2009, May 7, 2015, http://medical-dictionary.thefreedictionary.com/butyric+fermentation

[438]"Butyric acid", *Segen's Medical Dictionary*, 2012, accessed May 7, 2015, http://medical-dictionary.thefreedictionary.com/Butyric+acid+fermentation

depending on how hot or cool the climate is. And once the fluids of the body dry out, and when tissue in the organs has mostly decayed, then post decay takes over. This involves even more insects, beetles and flies, coming in and taking advantage of the hair, cartilage, and sticky byproducts left over from the decaying process.[439]

Now, what is left over after all of this, a year or two later, is a protein in the bones and teeth called hydroxyapatite. It gives bone and teeth rigidity and makes up the bone mineral.[440] This dissolves, the bone decomposes, and turns to dust. In this regard, in the long process of decomposition, lasting anywhere from one to two years, sometimes more if in colder climates, eventually we turn to "ashes to ashes; dust to dust."[441] This is, of course, only if we leave a body alone to decompose as any other would in the wilderness. When bodies are taken into funeral homes, embalming fluids can help slow down the process so they body can hang on to its composition for a while longer. But it is just as inevitable in this circumstance as one left to the whims of nature; eventually, we all become fertilizer.

Realizing the finality of it all, and understanding what happens to the human body once the life-preserving fluids and actions we are all used to cease, is rather depressing. To step back and realize that, not only is there no probability of an afterlife or even a soul, but also once we die we disappear after a few years, is a bitter pill to swallow. Sadly, we cannot make a reality like this one any less true, even if we wish it not to be. As

---

[439]"What Happens...", *Discovery News*, 2014

[440]"Hydroxyapatite", MedicineNet.com, August 28, 2013, accessed May 7, 2015, http://www.medicinenet.com/script/main/art.asp?articlekey=7368

[441]Fischetti, *Scientific American*, 2014

sad and uncomfortable as this thought may make us, there is still a bigger picture to help ease our concern and make us more comfortable with the thought of our lives ending.

The Light at the End of the Tunnel

We are all carbon based life forms. About 96-99% of our body, the human body, is made up of carbon, oxygen, hydrogen, and nitrogen.[442] In the human body, carbon is only second to oxygen in terms of being the most present element in our chemistry.[443] As a result, when we die, the bacteria in our bodies feast on the carbon within us and transform that into CO2, carbon dioxide. This can be avoided, or at least sped up, if a body is cremated, releasing carbon as CO2 upon incineration. Again, we are teetering back towards the depressing side of (non) life after death, but it is with this in mind that we can fully grasp the benefit of our deaths. Aside from the fact that there is one less person to use up natural resources, our bodies actually contribute to the life of other living things on the planet when we, or the cremator or bacteria, release the CO2 from within our bodies. That molecule is an essential nutrient for all photosynthetic life on the planet.[444]

This is not just specific to land plants; this is also inclusive of algae and plants living underwater as well. Carbon dioxide is

[442]Schirber, Michael, "the Chemistry of Life: the Human Body", *Live Science*, April 16, 2009, accessed May 11, 2015,
http://www.livescience.com/3505-chemistry-life-human-body.html
[443]"Biological abundance of elements", *Encyclopedia of Science*, October 9, 2008, accessed May 11, 2015,
http://www.daviddarling.info/encyclopedia/E/elbio.html
[444]Volk, Tyler, and Sagan, Dorion, *Death & Sex*, Chelsea Green Publishing, White River Junction, VT, 2009, pg. 21

certainly a gas found in our atmosphere, but when it dissolves it finds itself sinking into the water. Just as oxygen can dissolve and find its way into water, carbon dioxide does and can do it 200 times faster than oxygen. Plants underwater depend on CO2 and photosynthesis just as much as land plants do.[445] It is an almost 40/60 split between marine phytoplankton and land plants that require carbon dioxide for survival, and the human body gives almost all that these life forms require.[446]

Part of the carbon dioxide, both in the air and coming from decomposed or decomposing bodies, sinks and dissolves into the soil. After some time, this carbon reemerges into plant life and the atmosphere. This can be thought of as a sort of "resurrection," if you will, of our chemical makeup. When it does this, it can come up in a number of ways through the agonizingly slow process of the carbon cycle. One is through volcanic activity, which is, to some extent, the restart of the cycle: closing a 100 to 200 million-year process. In other words, after you die, 100 to 200 million years in the future your chemical makeup could be blown back into the atmosphere as a volcanic eruption.[447] So today, when a volcano erupts, we are witnessing the resurrection of the carbon that inhabited the bodies of the first species of bees, newts, starfish, hermit crabs, and salamanders, among a plethora of other animals, some still alive and some long since extinct, from the Mesozoic era.

---

[445]"Oxygen and Carbon Dioxide", *Michigan Sea Grant*, 2015, accessed May 11, 2015, http://www.miseagrant.umich.edu/lessons/lessons/by-broad-concept/earth-science/water-quality/oxygen-and-carbon-dioxide/
[446]Volk and Sagan, *Death & Sex*, pg. 24
[447]"The Slow Carbon Cycle", *NASA Earth Observatory*, 2015, accessed May 11, 2015, http://earthobservatory.nasa.gov/Features/CarbonCycle/page2.php

We should still keep a very real perspective on how we affect other bodies, after our death. Though the plant life absorbs and uses the CO2 that comes out of the earth, it is nowhere near the amount needed to sustain all plant life on the planet. Each year, 500 million tons of carbon dioxide comes up from within the earth and is taken in by plant life. But that is a fraction of a percentage that plant life uses; all plant life on the earth needs 100,000 million tons of carbon dioxide in order to survive. So resurrected carbon only makes up 0.5% of the total taken in by plants in order to survive.[448]

Care to guess where the remaining 99.5% of the CO2 needed comes from? Us. Well, more specifically, it comes from the water and air that has absorbed the CO2, but it originated in us.[449] Humans, and every other carbon based living, breathing, eating, digesting thing gives back to the planet what we take from it with our bodies. In an almost literal interpretation of *the Lion King's* "Circle of Life," it is the circle of life through carbon and carbon dioxide. Plants provide sustenance for animals (and humanity as well), those animals are eaten, or die naturally, and perhaps the predators (humans included) are eaten or die naturally. When they die, their carbon is eaten by bacteria that produce CO2. The CO2 is absorbed in the air and taken in by terrestrial plant life, or it dissolves into the waters and is taken in by aquatic plants. Or it is buried with the body and dissolves into the ground. The cycle repeats there, or the carbon goes through a 100 to 200 million year process where it reemerges into the atmosphere and is taken in by plants to start the carbon cycle once again.

---

[448]Volk and Sagan, *Death & Sex*, pg. 24-25
[449]Volk and Sagan, *Death & Sex*, pg. 25

So think about what we have just discussed: the planet is so strongly dependent on the carbon from our bodies when we die it is astounding. Not by a small fraction, but almost entirely reliant on the carbon that comes from us. It is not just a fact that we die, but a necessity. Again, as I had stated before, this is not my attempt to be an advocate for mass suicide. I am not saying that by any stretch of the imagination. However, when it comes down to our final moments on earth, prolonging it only makes it harder for us to let go and is denying what is an essential part of being alive. We all must die. And, as a result, we then become responsible for the next steps that lead into a new cycle of life. We become responsible for plant life, on land and at sea, which fuels the life of animals in both areas to survive. We continue to live by giving life to the next wave of whatever carbon based life follows us. And that is not only a good thing, it is a magnificently beautiful thing.

Conclusion

Science tells us a lot about what happens when we die. And, more importantly, it tells us what does *not* happen when we die. With the help of science, we can accurately show that those experiences of seeing deceased relatives, floating in a tunnel towards a bright light, or hovering over our own bodies during surgeries, are nothing more than natural neurological responses to stressful, or extreme, circumstances. And, more importantly, they can be replicated and studied. We can stimulate different aspects of a person's mind and cause them to experience what others would label an NDE, but science knows it to be a response to stress or other biological circumstances.

Those feelings of hauntings, a presence in a room, a hand on an individual's shoulder, or sense of being watched, can also be explained by natural phenomena. And those very same phenomena can set off tools used to search for ghosts. They are caused by car brakes, nocturnal animals, and other electronic devices. Tests have shown a huge reaction when similar circumstances are set up, even in a busy concert hall. So these claims by popular "ghost hunter" series on TV, books, and other media platforms can be dismissed due to the overwhelming evidence to demonstrate that these claims are false. And, while I could have dedicated a section to claims made by entertainers that they are capable of speaking to the dead, there is no need to, thanks to people far more qualified and dedicated to that line of work. James Randi, of the James Randi Educational Foundation, has posed a challenge to anyone who does paranormal tricks like, among others, talking to the dead "under satisfactory observation".[450] If they can perform the feat without Randi being capable of explaining it or copying it, then the contestant wins one million dollars. To date, no one has proven that any supernatural feats they can perform, including communications with the dead, are anything more than clever magic tricks.

On the subject of reincarnation, we know these claims to be equally problematic. Often they are claims made about people who are of high status or wealth, and the people making the claims are looking for an inheritance of some kind. Perhaps it is even to seek out a moment of fame, as numerous people make claims of being the reincarnated Jesus, Gandhi, or Marilyn

---

[450]"the Million Dollar Challenge", *the James Randi Educational Foundation*, 2015, accessed May 11, 2015, http://web.randi.org/the-million-dollar-challenge.html

Monroe.[451] It seems suspicious at best, but it also is easy to claim to remember past lives when certain individuals, especially celebrities and notable people of history, have such highly documented lives with easy access to the information. When a skeptical light is shone on the matter, it reveals that no such thing is happening, or ever did take place.

Even when matters of the soul arise, being a thing that is thought to be capable of being weighed, the study proves that anything but such a concept is the truth. Poor science done to "prove" a soul has weight, like in the experiments in the consumption house in Massachusetts, show a desperation to demonstrate what individuals *want* to be true. It ignores the legitimate science, and even the results from repeated, and failed, experiments replicating the one that produced the result the scientist was attempting to find. Using information to appeal to what we want to be true, and ignoring what contradicts our assumptions, is not just poor science, it is dishonesty parading as fact — a wolf in sheep's clothing, if you will. And if that is what a scientist feels is needed to get attention, and the beliefs they want out, then they are not a scientist that can be trusted. Much in the same way a teacher providing lessons on intelligent design, either instead of or alongside the theory of evolution, is a teacher that should not be trusted. How can we trust the people that give us information if, in fact, they are not giving the whole picture, or are providing complete lies?

Perhaps it all could be overlooked, or at least it could have been, until quantum mechanics, and quantum field theory,

---

[451]Radford, Benjamin, "the Reality of Reincarnation", *Live Science*, April 27, 2009, accessed May 12, 2015, http://www.livescience.com/7737-reality-reincarnation.html

arrived and completely took the wind out of the sails for the argument for even an agnostic position on the afterlife. We know how things work on a quantum level, thanks to this incredible, mind-blowing field of physics. Even more than that, we know how particles, waves, fields, photons, all these pieces work, not just on an individual level, but how they function with other fields, particles, and waves on the quantum level. Because of this, we can see all aspects of matter, visible and invisible, and how they react in relation to one another. If such a thing as a soul existed, or some version of the afterlife, we would have demonstrable evidence for it in quantum mechanics. And we do not. We have mathematic formulas to demonstrate how all this works with what we do know, in science, in physics — with matter and vibrations and all else. If we accepted the theory of the soul, the mathematic formula would not work with physics, and we would need to demonstrate how it would, or could, work. More than that, we would need to completely rewrite, and reevaluate, books on math, physics, and all other fields of science.

What it comes down to is this: there is no room for the concept of the soul and, by proxy, the afterlife in our understanding of the world. There is no need to remain agnostic; the evidence is clear. No scientific process has proven a link between death and a soul or afterlife. We have natural explanations for all the things we experience when we die, both from animal experiments and from neurological and biological processes and tests. And, when looked at on the quantum level, we see no evidence, or room, for something like a soul. And, if there is no soul, then there is no afterlife. If there is no afterlife, then there is no heaven, hell, supernatural Gehenna, Sheol, or anything else resembling a realm of the dead.

That is not to say we do not "live on," in some way or another. After we go through the, honestly, gruesome process of dying, the bacteria that eats away at our bodies, or the process of cremation, releases the carbon dioxide in our bodies into the atmosphere. When that happens, plant life, both on land and in the sea, take in that CO_2, and it is put back through the natural cycle of life. Plants become food for other life, both aquatic and terrestrial, and that life ends up dying at some point, and the cycle continues. Or, the CO_2 from our bodies dissolves into the earth and either reemerges in new plant life, as before, or it can go through the long process of the carbon cycle — eventually becoming part of a wild volcanic eruption, among other things, that expels our carbon back into the atmosphere to start the 100 to 200 million year process all over again.

It is not the most comforting picture to imagine; no one likes the thought of ceasing to exist and not being conscious. Perhaps it is an evolutionary trait that we naturally have in order to keep us alive. The other option is the apathetic approach, certainly common in antiquity, of going out hunting for food among dangerous game, or perhaps heading in to battle and thinking nonchalantly, "I am going to die anyway, so what does it matter?" It seems very likely that type of thinking would be antithetical to survival of the species. Again, it is conjecture, but the idea that these bad feelings arise as a defense mechanism does not seem unlikely given how uncomfortable the subject of, not only death, but even mortality itself is.

We have come a long way in our discussion, and we have covered a lot. But it is at this point that we need to discuss one last aspect: if we are now faced with the idea that the afterlife is not a real thing, how do we face our death and, perhaps, our own lives without it?

Chapter 7: Facing Death as a Non-Believer

When I started writing this book, I must admit, as much as I did not believe there to be an afterlife, I was still open to the idea that, perhaps, we just did not know enough to be able to tell. I did not believe there to be one, in other words, but I was open to the idea that there might have been a possibility. I very obviously did not know the science behind the concept, nor what we do know, or are capable of knowing. I would not call it naivety, but certainly ego. I am just as guilty of wishing for the possibility of life after death as any other person — believer and non-believer alike. However, the science shows a complete absence of any type of afterlife, and to deny that is to be dishonest. Going back to the idea of teachers giving false information, I am no teacher if I am knowingly providing inaccurate data.

To an extent, the feeling I received from discovering the fact that we are capable of knowing there is no life beyond life is very similar to the feeling I had once I realized the concept of God was not real. It was a feeling I had while reading Victor Stenger's *God: the Failed Hypothesis* — placing the book in my lap as I finished, mouth agape, staring into what felt like, quite literally, the void. It was not so much a sinking feeling, but a free falling one. I felt lost, out of touch, and was so far gone from the others I needed that I did not think anyone could offer the help I required.

I imagine it the way Sandra Bullock's character looked to have felt in the movie "Gravity" after her ship had been destroyed — the image of being alone and without support in a very real, very scary, circumstance. Well, as real as one can imagine a made up scenario in a Hollywood film. But doing my research, and writing this book, brought back twinges of those familiar feelings. It was certainly not to the same level, but I recognized it nonetheless. The finality of death is unappealing, and it is sad. When I am gone, I will no longer be conscious of the world around me, of myself (as I will no longer exist), or the feelings I enjoy. The memories of my daughter laughing as I carry her through the house buzzing like she is an airplane, playing "Legend of Zelda" games with my boys, talking with my wife and listening to our favorite nineties music late into the evening, and on, and on, and on. Once I am gone, not only do I go, but my memories and sensations go with me. Even writing this, I get emotional thinking about what I will miss, and what I will no longer experience, once I am gone.

And with this feeling in mind, it brings me to my first point, the more pertinent one. What do we do about our life here, on Earth, if we no longer have a life after this one? I have made a bit of a case for this in other sections; I do not, for instance, advocate for ending our lives in light of not having an afterlife. Nor do I think it is a rational, reasonable response. I have heard it asked numerous times and read a Free Thought Blog responding to claims that, with no belief in God, atheists have no life purpose, and should just kill themselves.[452] The answer is pretty simple: atheists do not kill themselves because we know this is the only life we have. Much like the author of the article

---

[452]"Why Don't Atheists Just Kill Themselves?" *Free Thought Blogs*, September 22, 2013, accessed May 12, 2015, http://freethoughtblogs.com/cuttlefish/2013/09/22/why-dont-atheists-just-kill-themselves/

mentioned states, I have a wife and children I love and do not wish to be without, and who I know depend on me as much as I depend on them. I love playing music, teaching, reading, learning, movies, coffee, writing, and millions of other things. While I am a person that does not subscribe to a supernatural belief, that is not the only part of me that defines my life.

While I cannot offer an objective "meaning of life," though I am partial to Monty Python's suggestion of being kind to one another, reading good books, and so on, I can offer a rather subjective view. We have no choice whether we are born or not, but we should count ourselves lucky that we were. Not to suggest our lives are miracles, as we are truly a product of the circumstances of our planet's growth and place in our solar system, and there are more than seven billion instances of human life as we speak, but think about the potential for human life. First, consider that, when your parents had intercourse, there were 250 million sperm cells released for the one egg that was present when your mother became pregnant.[453] You are, I think it is reasonable to argue, one in 250 million. You are you because your parents had intercourse at a specific moment in time where the sperm and egg that made up who you are came together.

Now, for a moment, imagine something had happened prior to your parents deciding to have intercourse at the moment they did. Maybe the phone rang, or a Jehovah's Witness came to the door. Maybe your mother stubbed her toe on the leg of the bed and needed a moment to recuperate. If your parents had not

---

[453]Olson, Eric R., "Why Are 250 Million Sperm Cells Released During Sex?", *Live Science*, January 24, 2013, accessed May 12, 2015, http://www.livescience.com/32437-why-are-250-million-sperm-cells-released-during-sex.html

decided to have intercourse at the exact time that they did, you, very plausibly, could be someone else. More than that, you might not even exist. I do not mean to present this to then go in to a discussion of consciousness, sense of self, etc., but it brings up a crucial point. Because of an act, at a very specific moment, a particular sperm had an advantage to reach a particular egg, and out of that act with those two variables came you.[454] The individual that is reading this book, or hearing about it second hand — you, as an individual, had an almost zero percent chance of being here, and being conscious. Yet, here you are. Is that not remarkable in itself?

I could argue that humanity, as a whole, is relatively remarkable. I could also argue that life on our planet, all life that we see around us, is rare and remarkable. It is, but once we get past how amazing it is that there is life on this one planet, one that is on the outer rim of the galaxy of which we are a part, with no signs of life, as far as we can tell, close by, even with the probabilities of life. The Drake equation, a mathematical concept written up by astronomer Frank Drake in 1961 to determine the probability of life in the universe, shows that today, by conservative estimates, there is only one planet that is capable of communication in our galaxy (I would assume that would be us), and 78 billion in the entire universe.[455]

---

[454]This is a discussion taken, though roughly paraphrased, from Dr. Shelly Kagan's course on death, from Yale University's open courses. It is one that I used for reference in several places during this book and would highly encourage anyone to check out here: http://oyc.yale.edu/philosophy/phil-176

[455]"Drake equation: How many alien civilizations exist?", *BBC*, August 21, 2012, accessed May 12, 2015, http://www.bbc.com/future/story/20120821-how-many-alien-worlds-exist

Our species is not the only one in the universe, or perhaps the galaxy, but we are one among thousands, perhaps millions, of species that do live, or have lived, on our planet. Our species, among many others, is remarkable because we have this beautiful feature called consciousness. It is not a soul, nothing that helps us outlive our bodies, but it does give us the ability to be aware of life, ourselves, and our surroundings, in a way that is truly remarkable. It is something we truly take for granted, but when realized creates a sense of awe. How fortunate are we to be able to be aware, to reason, to argue, to offer counterpoint, negotiate, and to learn! How incredible it is that we have moved beyond a hunter-gatherer phase of existence into one where we learn about our environment, ourselves, our prey and predators, how life works, how our bodies work, and to do things to prolong our lives and enjoy them for longer. With the technological, or information, age came a growth in human life expectancy. At the beginning of the last century, our expected lifespan was about 31 years. In 2005, it was 65.6, and in 2030, the projected life expectancy from birth will be 85 years.[456] If there is nothing else to consider for why we should want, and love, to live despite there being no afterlife, it is because of the good we are capable of doing for others by learning and understanding as much as we can. This is why I spend so much time reading books, listening to lectures, and talking with friends who are knowledgeable in different areas than I; I long to know as much as I can so that I can combine my knowledge to create

---

[456]Prentice, Thomas, "Health, history, and hard choices: Funding dilemmas in a fast-changing world", *World Health Organization*, August 2006, accessed May 12, 2015,
http://www.who.int/global_health_histories/seminars/presentation07.pdf

opportunities to help educate others, to find new resources, discover new ways of thinking, all in order to help better the lives of others. Even in the most simple of acts, a little can go a long way.

Perhaps I am getting long-winded at this point, and maybe I need to focus my point a little. So, to help demonstrate why my philosophy is one that champions living a gracious, positive life, I need to speak of my own experiences, rather than putting everything in a microcosm, or macrocosm.

Given the story I revealed at the beginning of the book, of my heart attack, I like to think I was given a second opportunity to experience life. Not given by an immaterial, cosmic deity, but by the nurse at my school, my father, and the EMTs who prevented me from dying. After the event, growing up, the struggle became difficult between my parents and me. I was not an easy child to get along with, and I certainly had difficulty taking points seriously and understanding the consequences of my actions at times. From my perspective, I saw I had experienced circumstances that were too close to death in order to take life seriously. I had to go out and seize every moment — take every opportunity to live a great life and have plenty of stories to tell when I am older (I assumed the word "if" replaced "when" in many instances). It did not matter to me that I did not have my medication when I went to a concert in Montreal when I was 18. How often did a band I love come so near to my home where no large acts came through? It was of little concern, at the time, that I almost failed the one math class I needed to graduate from high school. I had far more fun bribing my classmate with pledged dollars to skip around the classroom when the teacher had her back turned to us, rather than taking note of what she was saying.

While my care-free attitude worked well for me, and certainly made my life enjoyable at the time, my parents were on the other end of the spectrum. My life was too precious to be so careless, and I was blind to their concern. My father worried more than any other and, looking back, I am horrified to see what he went through with me and how I reacted to his concern. A few years after my incident, he was at a local fitness club teaching a CPR class when a young man, no more than a few years older than I, fell unconscious while exercising. He fell victim to the same heart complication (fibrillation) that I had, only he never woke up. My father administered CPR to him, making every attempt to bring him back, but to no avail. The poor young man died right in front of him. In retrospect, I am pretty embarrassed to admit I was such a problem child for my parents — adding to the already mounted concern they had for me by being care-free to the point of being care-less.

Of course, being that I was more interested in living an interesting and opportunistic life, I had many incredible experiences. I joined a band a year or so out of college, signed to an independent record label, released an album, and toured the country. I was able to do something pretty incredible, play for some amazing audiences and other notable bands, and saw some great parts of the country. I would not have had the opportunity to see and do these things had I not taken the risk that came with being in a band, and relying on the kindness of strangers to help feed us, put gas in our touring van, and get us to the next city. When I had another opportunity to record with an unsigned band, it meant traveling to Chicago, spending two weeks in a studio owned by a well-known musician, working with producers who had fabulous careers, one even being a GRAMMY Award winner, and doing a professionally-recorded album. This was something that had been a dream of mine, and today still seems surreal, because I opted to be a little careless and to take a risk.

These risks, however, did not come without consequences. With the first band, I let my ego get in the way and I treated four individuals, who I felt were family, like absolute dirt at times. I put a lot of money into investments I saw no return on, and my actions left me with a rather bad reputation in the small music community I was a part of. The other act I became involved with replaced me a few short weeks after we finished the recording because I became ill and could not tour. I received no recognition for the work and contribution I put into the record I made with them, and, again, all financial investments were never returned, despite the album selling as well as they alleged. Stories, it seems, are all I have left to show for what I took part in.

It was from these experiences, as well as a failing economy and music business, that I knew I needed to take my drive and ambition elsewhere. I entered a graduate program in theology at my alma mater, and opted to go in a more academic route. I did this because I knew I had a passion, and a way of explaining things to others, that triggered something similar to what I felt in myself. I did it, first, through music. I had a young student who came to me with a basic version of the Star Wars theme song, by John Williams. He was still relatively new at the instrument, and he struggled, but he was eager to learn. When I was able to show him an easy way to play, he lit up. He was beside himself with joy, expressing his eagerness to show off his new skill to his parents. And, what moved me the most, was that he attributed his newfound capability to how I taught him. He explained to me that he would not have been able to learn it without my help.

I have seen similar reactions from people who do not know certain things about the Bible, about history, and about how the messages became scrambled over two millennia. When I make blog posts about theology, or the history of the early church, I sometimes receive comments or statements from people who say they had no clue about an issue until I explained it. One of my now close working relationships, and an individual I am ever grateful to have, is with JD Brucker, the author of *Improbable: Problems with the God Hypothesis.* He first reached out to me after reading my blog, explaining he had learned a lot from me.

My point in all this is to emphasize my own perspective on life, not only without religion, but without the belief in, and now knowledge of, an afterlife. I look back on the mistakes I have made in life and cringe; I know from my own experience that these things are not actions I would take part in today, but I know that *because* I went through these experiences. My belief, or even hope, in an afterlife had little to do with my decisions, as I was more conscious, and (despite my actions) concerned with my mortality. In all the decisions I have made, since the incident, the frailty of my life has always been front and center. Over time, however, that concern moved from "I need good stories to tell" to "I need to make sure I survive to actually tell the stories."

My experiences are my own, and they are certainly right for what I was capable of and willing to do. For me, even acknowledging that the afterlife is more likely myth than truth, made the desire to live and lead a happy and healthy life stronger. But, part of the point I am attempting to make is that I was held accountable for my actions. Not having an afterlife does not make us responsible for the actions we take part in, and this is because we have a system in place to provide consequences when poor decisions are made. Parts of them are cultural; if someone's significant other is unfaithful to them, instead of overlooking it, there is an emotional trigger and, in some cases, there is a separation. Or, at the very least, there is a bottom line sent where a reform of actions needs to happen or a separation will. To a higher degree, if someone commits a crime, like murder, regardless of their religious beliefs they will face a judge and jury, and potentially jail time.

A prime example is Craig Stephen Hicks, the man charged with killing three Muslims in the Chapel Hill shootings.[457] There is some dispute over what caused the initial confrontation, but there are some definite points we can take from this, at least for our purposes. First, Hicks is an atheist; he does not believe in any supernatural deities and, as some suggest, there is a possibility he was an anti-theist, one who is opposed to all forms of religious belief and practice. This definition is not absolutely perfect, but it gives you the general gist of the idea behind it. Second, Hicks committed a horrendous act by taking the lives of three people. Regardless of the circumstances, the conflict is one that very likely could have, and should have, ended without any blood being spilled, let alone from three people. Hicks is not only facing prison time, but the judge determined that he is "death penalty qualified."[458] To any theist who may make the claim that atheists do not believe so that they can sin, and not be held responsible for their actions: there are still consequences for horrible decisions. And, again, this is regardless of an individual's personal religious beliefs.

---

[457]"Craig Stephen Hicks", *Huffington Post*, http://www.huffingtonpost.com/news/craig-stephen-hicks/
[458]Biesecker, Michael, and Drew, Jonathan, "Craig Hicks Can Face Death Penalty In Chapel Hill Muslim Killings, Judge Rules", *Huffington Post*, April 6, 2015, accessed May 13, 2015, http://www.huffingtonpost.com/2015/04/06/craig-hicks-death-penalty-muslim-killings_n_7013700.html

To illustrate the larger point I am making, I offer the scene from the 1993 movie "Philadelphia" with Tom Hanks and Denzel Washington. For those who have not seen it, the movie is based in part on a case surrounding attorney Geoffrey Bowers who sued his law firm for similar circumstances that the lead, Tom Hanks, in "Philadelphia" encountered.[459] The particular scene I am referring to happens prior to Hanks' character, Andrew Beckett, going to testify in court against the law firm that fired him, allegedly due to his medical affliction, AIDS. He is seated with his lawyer, Joe Miller played by Denzel Washington, and stops him during part of an opera record he has playing. After telling Miller it is his favorite aria, he stands up, his emaciated frame being supported by him pulling on the stand holding his IV. He turns up the volume and translates what the singer is saying, accenting the various points by stating how changes to the music help the emotion of the piece evolve. During the climax of the song, Hanks translates the singing as "Live still, I am life. Heaven is in your eyes. Is everything around you just the blood and mud? I am divine. I am oblivion. I am the god... that comes down from the heavens, and makes of the Earth a heaven. *I am love*! I am love."

When Hanks' character realizes the song is over, Miller concedes that he is ready for trial and leaves. When Miller gets home, he goes into his daughter's room, picking her up, only a few months old, he embraces and calms her as she starts to fuss.

---

[459]Pristin, Terry, "What Is The Story Behind The 'Philadelphia' Story?: Movies: A lawsuit alleging the film's idea is based on a real case has aroused curiosity about the origins of the TriStar feature.', *Los Angeles Times*, February 17, 1994, accessed May 13, 2015, http://articles.latimes.com/1994-02-17/entertainment/ca-24208_1_bowers-family

After a moment, he places her back in bed, and goes to his wife, asleep as well. He climbs in next to her, still clothed in his suit, and puts his arm around her, only to have her return the affection. Miller does not cry, he does not cower, he does not even pray. Instead, he realizes what is most important in his life at that time and takes an opportunity, perhaps one his character would have normally missed, and soaked himself in it. He, very literally, saw a man who was facing his death, in the 1980s when AIDS was nothing short of a terminal condition. And when he realized this, and saw how Beckett embraced his life, or what may have been left of it, it appears to have made him reflective of his own mortality. So when he had an opportunity to embrace the things that made him human, that made him a living, breathing, conscious being, he took the chance. No conversions, no praying, begging, negotiating, or calling on some supernatural powers; he saw death, he realized how frail humanity is, and he took a moment to envelop himself in what made him feel alive. Just like Andrew Beckett did with the aria.

We are faced, daily, with numerous ways to perish. A car accident could take us while we are stopped in traffic, we could choke on a bit of food we did not chew thoroughly, we could fall down stairs, or there could even be an asteroid impact that strikes and kills us.[460] The fact is that, daily, we face innumerable ways in which we could die. Still, we live in a comfortable bubble that lets us believe that it will not happen to us — that we are invincible. Yet I, and many like myself, are well aware that, not only is it probable that something out of the ordinary could potentially happen to cause my death, truly at any time,

---

[460] "Daily chart: Danger of death", *the Economist*, February 14, 2013, accessed May 13, 2015,
http://www.economist.com/blogs/graphicdetail/2013/02/daily-chart-7

there is also nothing more to experience once that death does happen. What we have now, in this mortal life, is it.

Conclusion

My philosophy, in narrowing down everything to the bare essentials, is this: know that you are going to die. Know that it is not a pretty thing when you die, and that the time you do have is, not only short, but wholly priceless. We can never get back moments that are lost, never relive moments when we feel we were at our happiest, but also, fortunately, times when we were at our lowest points. It does matter to live in the present moment, but it also matters how you plan out those moments for the future.

If we are set on a plan of self-fulfillment, and self-satisfaction, we are doomed to make mistakes and lose close acquaintances, as well as prospects for sustaining the good in our lives for the long run. If you end up burning bridges, in other words, you will have fewer opportunities to go back in order to seek, or find, other paths to benefit yourself. So, when making plans in your life, ensure there is a greater good that comes from said plans — a good beyond helping yourself.

We also need to understand that we will also never have a chance to get back those little moments we pass up, the embrace, offer of affection, greeting, even saying "I love you" to those we cherish. Every night I go to sleep, I do my best to ensure that, before hand, I give each of my children and wife a hug, kiss, and an "I love you." While I am sure, when I am on my death bed, I will feel it was not enough, but I would rather go knowing I made every effort to make sure my family knew I loved them rather than making them guess. Actions speak louder than words, and the more we act on them, the more we will be heard and fewer questions will be asked.

Lastly, we need to realize what makes us who we are. I am who I am through my family, first and foremost, then my friends, music, books and writing, the food I love to cook and eat, and on and on. I ensure that I spend adequate time with the ones I care about, participating in activities that they enjoy (as exhausting as I find playing the airplane game for long periods of time, the laughter I get to hear from my daughter makes up for any discomfort by all accounts), making food they love, and just giving them my time. I play music for myself and my family, learning songs they enjoy, playing games with music, or just talking about music, even if it is a memory of a concert or musician that is no longer around. These are all what make me who I am, and this is what helps me feel alive and important. My view is that others should follow suit and embrace what makes them happy, even if it means sacrificing a bit of happiness, or yourself, if it brings joy to you in another way.

And, just to be clear, bringing joy to one's self does not mean bringing misery to others. Though we must consider our own lives, we also have to consider how we leave the world for those we leave behind. I would not take my family's savings and spend it all to ensure I leave the world a happier person. That might leave my family destitute and in a much worse condition. Similarly, just because someone enjoys hunting does not mean they should shoot at everything that appears to be moving, and then not feel any remorse when they hit another human who is out hunting the same day, in the same location. This is why there are consequences in place to prevent such actions, and a cultural consequence built from how our species evolved over the hundreds of thousands of years it has been around. Self-satisfaction does not mean zero satisfaction, or misery, for all else. We need reasonable, and moral, boundaries.

The very center of my argument is that it is not the same for all, and so the values and opinions change. This is why, when considering our mortality, we need to understand how our actions affect those around us in the world. As non-believers in an afterlife, there needs to be, and I am of the opinion that there very much is, an emphasis on leading a good life, a moral life, in the present. People need to be held accountable for what happens while they are here, and how they contribute to the world during that time. If people are threatening, or harming, people of different faiths, women who make choices with their bodies that go against a group's teachings, or people who are of the LGBTQ persuasion, then we need to deliver consequences for those beliefs and actions. Even on a verbal level, there are scars that cannot be healed or erased from verbal abuse because of a difference of opinion or beliefs. Those who identify as non-believers need to make attempts to argue against such repugnant, prejudiced views. And that starts with speaking out, and speaking up.

Epilogue

I started this book, unbeknownst to me, as part of my graduate thesis. During the time I studied theology, I was no longer a believer, and so was unsurprised by a lot of what I discovered in the biblical text, but it still struck me as fascinating. How curious it was, seeing so little of the beliefs we hold today in the ancient texts of Judaism, and the beginnings of Christianity. How curious, indeed, to see it develop through the centuries — with varying views and changing beliefs due to cultural circumstances.

What becomes all the more fascinating is how, even in a philosophical light, the idea of an afterlife becomes nothing short of preposterous. If the soul exists, how does that work with my level of consciousness? Do we have the same soul our entire lives? How do we prove that? How do we prove the immortality of an immaterial thing? What kind of life is an acceptable one when we reach the afterlife? Is it enough to be conscious? To be mobile? To have choice? If we do not have all these things, and we are supposed to be in a heavenly afterlife, is that something we can truly consider paradise? These questions, among many others, show that the concept of an afterlife seems improbable, if not impossible, and they are merely asked as part of a thought experiment.

When we get to the realm of science, however, the story changes completely. We find evidence that things like reincarnation are nothing short of attempts to find small amounts of fame, and potentially to gain wealth from a family that lost someone they love. Hauntings are not much more than a result of natural echoes being emitted by animals, vehicles, and electronics, among other natural, explainable, phenomena. NDEs are natural, biological and neurological, stimulations that happen under stress or when bodily harm occurs or is risked. And, when seen at the quantum level, there is no room for such nonsense as the idea of an "immaterial" soul. If such a thing existed, we would have evidence for it, and no such thing has been found. Through proxy, it is more than reasonable to then assume there is no realm for the dead to reside in. If there are no souls, then there is no need for such a place to exist.

So what purpose does this book serve, other than to demonstrate a lack of life beyond life, reasons to question the biblical account, or show our cultures separation from it, and to, hopefully, offer perspective, insight, and hope for those coming to terms with there being no afterlife? Simple: this, death, is one of the main reasons people of any faith are divided against atheists.

At the time of writing, through some amazing matter of serendipity, the news site Vice released an article titled "Atheism Terrifies People because It Makes Us Think About Death." In this article, the author says studies have demonstrated that, not only are the devoutly religious intent on demonstrating that the non-believers will suffer in hell, they also fear the same happening to people that they love. Corey Cook, a social psychologist at the University of Washington who performed a study called "What if They're Right About the Afterlife? Evidence of the Role of Existential Threat on Anti-Atheist Prejudice," has a theory called the "terror-management theory." His idea is, as noted in this book, that people are absolutely fearful of their own death, and that fear is subsided by the idea of a universal belonging through different cultural and religious groups.

From his study, Cook noticed a few things. First was that, on a conscious level, death made people appreciate life more and thinking about death can be a great thing for making people react in such a way. However, across the board, regardless of religious or non-religious views, it makes people look to and for those who support their world view, increasing in negative sentiments towards those who hold contrary beliefs and views. Atheists are not immune to this reaction, as Cook's study suggests. So it seems to imply that, with the thought of death looming in our minds, humans makes a great effort to segregate themselves, and people of similar mindsets and values, from those in opposition to them.

Though it is all a matter of acknowledging that we are all the same, to a degree, and will all meet the same fate, regardless of race, creed, sexuality, status, etc., it is more important to understand what those thoughts and feelings become when we are closer to death. While I had a taste of death, mine was not an instance of the finality of death. Prior to his death, author Christopher Hitchens, diagnosed with esophageal cancer, wrote some articles for *Vanity Fair* on his illness and coming to terms with his mortality. He writes,

> "*I have been taunting the Reaper into taking a free scythe in my direction and have now succumbed to something so predictable and banal that it bores even me. Rage would be beside the point for the same reason. Instead, I am badly oppressed by a gnawing sense of waste. I had real plans for my next decade and felt I'd worked hard enough to earn it. Will I really not live to see my children married? To watch the World Trade Center rise again? To read— if not indeed write—the obituaries of elderly villains like Henry Kissinger and Joseph Ratzinger? But I understand this sort of non-thinking for what it is: sentimentality and self-pity. Of course my book hit the best-seller list on the day that I received the grimmest of*

news bulletins, and for that matter the last flight I took as a healthy-feeling person (to a fine, big audience at the Chicago Book Fair) was the one that made me a million-miler on United Airlines, with a lifetime of free upgrades to look forward to. But irony is my business and I just can't see any ironies here: would it be less poignant to get cancer on the day that my memoirs were remaindered as a box-office turkey, or that I was bounced from a coach-class flight and left on the tarmac? To the dumb question "Why me?" the cosmos barely bothers to return the reply: Why not? "[461]

So why not us? The same can be turned around to offer perspective; we were given the chance nearly no other planet, that we are aware of, was given in our galaxy. Why was our planet given life? Does the cosmos offer the same reply? We are a product of four and a half billion years of development. Up to now, the result is us. In another million years, perhaps the life forms that inhabit our planet will ask the same. Or, perhaps, they will know the answer. At that point, the atoms that make up our bodies will have gone only a small percentage of the way into the circle of carbon recycling that the planet has performed only a few dozen times. We will have provided life to countless plant and animal beings that came after us, and perhaps something we were a small part of would show some benefit to help sustain life to the level it will reach a million years away. So when we look the cold face of death in the eyes, and we realize there is nothing beyond that point, we should not look back and say "why me," but instead "why not me."

---

[461] Hitchens, Christopher, "Topic of Cancer", *Vanity Fair,* August 2010, accessed May 13, 2015,
http://www.vanityfair.com/culture/2010/09/hitchens-201009

Matthew O'Neil

Index